ONCE UPON A FOLKTALE

CAPTURING THE FOLKLORE PROCESS WITH CHILDREN

Edited by
Gloria T. Blatt

TEACHERS COLLEGE PRESS

TEACHERS COLLEGE, COLUMBIA UNIVERSITY
NEW YORK AND LONDON

Published by Teachers College Press, 1234 Amsterdam Avenue, New York, NY 10027

The cover illustration of *Once Upon A Folktale* has been reproduced from the cover drawing of the *Rip Van Winkle Coloring Book* (an entry in the Dover Pictorial Archive Series), rendered by Pat Stewart after illustrations by Arthur Rackham; published in 1983 by Dover Publications, Inc. 180 Varick Street, New York, NY 10014.

Library of Congress Cataloging-in-Publication Data

Once upon a folktale : capturing the folklore process with children/ edited by Gloria T. Blatt.
   p.   cm.
Includes bibliographical references and index.
ISBN 0-8077-3232-X (alk. paper) : $18.95
   1. Folklore and children.   2. Folklore—Study and teaching (Elementary)   I. Blatt, Gloria T., 1924–   .
GR43.C4053   1933
398′.083—dc20   92-36897

ISBN 0-8077-3232-X

Printed on acid-free paper
Manufactured in the United States of America
98 97 96 95 95 94 93   8 7 6 5 4 3 2 1

CONTENTS

Introduction: Children and Folklore

Gloria T. Blatt

Long ago, when I was a child, my grandfather often entertained our family with stories of his childhood. According to him, his father was a baron who owned an imposing mansion in Baden-Baden, a German gambling center. His descriptions suggested that in his boyhood he had a life well beyond anything we had ever experienced in southern Ohio, for he said his father owned a stable of horses and employed numerous servants and private tutors, and that the family often went on trips to the local spa.

Even though we all knew that the stories were, at best, half truths, "small exaggerations," according to our grandmother, my cousins and I pranced around the busy kitchen holding forks like lorgnettes while we directed servants who did not exist. In a hilarious mood, we acted out the stories, exaggerating all the more because we knew all too well that they were not true.

To this day, I remember those afternoons with pleasure, as do my cousins. When we get together, we laugh about the tall tales Grandpa told. Never mind that the stories did not always fit together or that they differed from telling to telling. Half the fun lay in the way he changed them. Grandpa kept us spellbound, and we see this fascination in our children when we tell them our own versions of the same stories.

I also remember the rhymes and fairy tales that my mother told my brother and me. Like her father, she knew an endless number of stories; like him, she changed them again and again. The stories my mother told were often well-known tales like "Goldilocks and the Three Bears," "Cinderella," "Snow White and the Seven Dwarfs," "Sleeping Beauty," and the like. When she grew tired of storytelling, she often ended with, "There was a little girl who had a little curl right in the middle of her forehead. When she was good, she was very, very good; and when she was bad, she was horrid." I

1

knew then, just as my own daughter does now, that this little rhyme signaled time for bed.

My teachers continued the process begun by my family of introducing me to folklore by telling me fairy tales, and it was in school that I heard the Greek and Roman myths for the first time. I especially loved "Pandora's Box" and "Demeter and Persephone"; and to this day I am delighted when I come across them.

Often, as I played with other children during hot summer nights, I listened to and recited jokes and rhymes that are variants of ones that I hear children recite today:

> I scream, you scream,
> We all scream for ice cream.

or

> One for the money,
> Two for the show,
> Three to make ready,
> And four to go.

Such was the rich folklore heritage that I brought with me when I started school; such were the stories I later heard from my teachers. All serve me well to this day.

Rich as my experiences are and were, they were in no way unique. Boys and girls, and men and women, come in contact with folklore all the time. They hear "Mother Goose" and other nursery rhymes from their parents; they recite variations of jump-rope jingles and counting-out rhymes like

> One potato, two potato
> three potato, four
> Five potato, six potato
> Seven potato more.

or scary rhymes like

> Did you ever hear as the hearse rolls by
> That some of these days you must surely die?

with their friends. They listen to relatives telling family stories and snicker over old jokes and riddles that they think are brand new and that they change to suit themselves as they retell them. They love old fairy tales or myths and even relish urban tales that are calculated to terrify their listeners. They are surrounded by traditional literature. And people enjoy all of this without discrimination. Proof of their interest lies in the way they ask for more or sit stone still, seemingly spellbound, when someone obliges. Proof also lies in the way they themselves participate in the folklore process, retelling jokes, riddles, stories, and songs that they have heard elsewhere.

But even though all of us, young and old, relish experiences with the oral tradition, the reasons why children are fascinated with folklore have not always been clear. Some say that young people enjoy folklore because the stories are like their own daydreams. After all, every boy likes to imagine that he might win a kingdom, every girl that she might win a prince. Others say that the smooth, seamless stories, the predictable plots, the stereotypical characters, and the rhymes and songs that are so easily learned, play a part in children's delight. There is, after all, a certain pleasure in hearing a highly predictable story with a rhyme that is easily learned. Still others theorize that children enjoy such stories and rhymes so much because they are perfectly suited to their development. Although this last group of theorists approaches the topic in a variety of ways, their arguments are surprisingly similar.

The Russian poet Kornei Chukovsky (1963) argued that folklore meets the deep-seated needs of children. When the communist government of the Soviet Union forbade teachers to use folklore in their work with children, Chukovsky pointed out that, deprived of lore, children would invent rhymes and tales similar to traditional ones because these stories meet their emotional needs.

Peter and Iona Opie (1959) surveyed jump-rope jingles and other rhymes that children invent themselves and repeat when playing. The researchers described selected variants and pointed out that the rhymes reflect the children's developmental needs. Between 5 and 7 years of age young people often recite jingles like

> Eeny, meany, miney, mo,
> Sit the baby on the po.
> When he's done,
> Wipe his bum,
> Shove the paper up the lum. (p. 96)

because they are concerned with bodily functions and want to test linguistic taboos. Before adolescence, when the perils of sex and gender become personal issues, preadolescent girls often recite rhymes like

> Ivy, Ivy, I love you,
> In my bosom I put you.
> The first young man who speaks to me,
> My future husband he shall be. (p. 337)

or tell urban stories like "The Hook" because they are afraid of the changes occurring in their own bodies and the dangers lurking in the adult world:

> After the movies, Mike and Judy, two young people on a date, park on "Lover's Lane" on an isolated hill overlooking town. When they are well settled, the boy turns on the radio to listen to soft music. Suddenly, a newscaster breaks in to announce that an armed murderer has escaped from the state prison for the criminally insane and that he has a hook in place of a missing left hand.
>
> Because Judy is afraid, they decide to go home. Just as the car begins to roll down the hill, Judy thinks that she hears something scratching at the door.
>
> "Did you hear that?" she asks as they roar away. "It sounded like somebody trying to get in."
>
> At her house, Judy invites Mike in; but, still angry, he says, "No, I'm too busy." He goes around to the other side of the car to let her out. On the door is a hook. (A version of this story is recorded in Brunvand, 1981.)

In other words, the folklore that the children transmit becomes one of several psychological proving grounds that youngsters use to test social limits and to prepare themselves for transitions in their lives.

Bruno Bettleheim (1976), the psychiatrist, came to a similar conclusion after analyzing the psychological meaning of fairy tales. He concluded that the old stories express the children's own feelings. In Bettleheim's words,

> In order to master the psychological problems of growing up—overcoming narcissistic disappointments, sibling rivalry, relinquishing childhood dependencies, gaining a feeling of selfhood and self-worth, and a sense of moral obligation—a child needs to understand what is going on within his conscious self so that he can also cope with that which goes on in his unconscious. (p. 6)

Andre Favat (1977) theorized that, like the old tales, the minds of young people between the ages of 8 and 10 reflect a belief in enchantment, a faith that events can be changed by magic. Children are therefore not surprised to learn that Sleeping Beauty was unchanged after a hundred years of enchanted sleep or that her true love could wake her with a magic kiss. The stories "embody an accurate representation of the child's concept of the world" (p. 38).

Many teachers realize that folklore fits the intellectual and emotional development of children; they sense that youngsters use it to work through issues associated with growing up, so they want to take full advantage of all that folklore offers. Even when pressured to teach a dizzying array of required subjects, these teachers somehow manage to find time for folklore even in a busy class schedule.

But teachers miss an important element of folklore because all too often they think of traditional literature as an icon to be preserved exactly as it has come down to us. Like E. D. Hirsch (1987), they argue that children should be exposed to fairy tales like "Sleeping Beauty," "Snow White," and "Cinderella," as well as myths like Homer's *Iliad* and *Odyssey* because these and other folktales are keys to Western culture. Some, like Northrop Frye (1964), professor of literature at University of Toronto, even see folklore as a vehicle for understanding literature:

> If we don't know the Bible and the central stories of Greek and Roman ... [folklore], we can still read books and see plays, but our knowledge of literature cannot grow, just as our knowledge of mathematics can't grow if we don't know the multiplication table. (pp. 48–49)

Important as they are, the comments of Hirsch and Frye have their limitations. If we adhere to their ideas entirely, we will not be able to take full advantage of folklore, and all that it offers children, for a number of reasons.

First, although folklore is a key to understanding literature, it is not the same as literature by known writers. Authors may draw on folklore sources, but they produce works of art that should not be changed once completed. Folklore, on the other hand, is always changing, always in flux. As people pass tales by word of mouth from person to person, they change the stories and poems to suit themselves. There is therefore no single "right" way to tell a story or recite a rhyme. By presenting folklore as a collection of completed stories and rhymes that must not be changed, teachers mistake the nature of folklore.

Second, children are actively involved in using folklore from the moment their mothers begin to tell them "Mother Goose" rhymes or sing them lullabies. They recite jump-rope jingles, tell jokes and riddles, and try out rap or whatever is popular. It therefore makes good sense for teachers to take full advantage of the real connection between folklore and children.

This book is designed for exactly that purpose. It deals with ways to bring children and lore together in a lively, interactive fashion that taps the folklore process and the way children use it. Teachers will learn how to take full advantage of interests youngsters already have and to use folklore to understand literature more deeply; they will also learn how to empower youngsters to become storytellers and to guide them as they learn how to record folklore and write their own variants. Above all, the teachers will learn how to tap folktales to empower their children as storytellers and writers of folklore. The results will be satisfying for teachers and children alike.

REFERENCES

Bettleheim, B.(1976). *The uses of enchantment: The meaning and importance of fairy tales.* New York: Knopf.

Brunvand, J.(1981). *The vanishing hitchhiker.* New York: Norton.

Chukovsky, K.(1963). *From two to five.* Translated by Miriam Morton. Berkeley: University of California Press.

Favat, A.(1977). *Child and tale: The origins of interest* (NCTE Report No. 19). Urbana, IL: National Council of Teachers of English.

Frye, N.(1964). *The educated imagination.* Bloomington: Indiana University Press.

Hirsch, E. D., Jr. (1987). *Cultural literacy.* Boston: Houghton Mifflin.

Opie, P., & Opie, I. (1959). *The lore and language of children.* New York: Oxford University Press.

PART I

🌸 BRINGING FOLKLORE AND CHILDREN TOGETHER IN SCHOOL: A BEGINNING

Teachers do all they can to introduce pupils to folklore. They read and tell fairy tales, they ask their charges to read others, and then introduce youngsters to Greek and Roman myths. But rarely do they take full advantage of the folklore that already runs like a rich vein through the lives of the children in their classes.

Part I is a treasure trove of strategies for quarrying that mother lode. The chapters in this section will help teachers take full advantage through storytelling, reading, and writing of the folklore background that children bring to elementary classrooms. In addition, each chapter is followed by a practical classroom strategy entitled "Try This," a teaching guide that grows directly out of the preceding chapter.

CHAPTER 1

🌿 TELLING STORIES: A KEY TO READING AND WRITING

R. Craig Roney

Obviously, storytellers are pivotal figures in the folklore process. Many mesmerize audiences who sit stone still, caught up in the performance. They, in turn, then pass their own versions of the same or similar stories along to others.

Teachers are well aware of the power inherent in telling stories. Although many make a special point of bringing storytellers to their classes, they themselves may be reluctant to tell tales because they are anxious about their own performances, unsure how to use storytelling as a teaching tool. They thereby miss an important opportunity.

In the chapter that follows, Craig Roney, well-known storyteller and professor of children's literature, outlines ways teachers can make use of storytelling: how to use stories to enhance learning, how to select easy-to-learn tales, and how to learn them. He includes practical guides for teaching, bibliographies for beginning storytellers, and suggestions for empowering pupils as storytellers and writers.

If folklore is the oldest form of literature, then storytelling may be the oldest medium of education. It dates back to the dawn of civilization when our ancient ancestors wove their beliefs, knowledge, mores, and history into tales and then transmitted their collective wisdom from one person (or group of persons) to another, one generation to the next, via the oral tradition. Today storytelling retains its prominence as a major means of acculturation in many nonindustrialized countries and in subcultures within industrialized nations. Telling stories is also gaining in popularity as a

9

medium of instruction in our own schools due, in part, to the whole language movement.

Storytelling can be used in the classroom in two ways: as a means of acculturation or edification and/or as an aid to developing literacy in students. Whereas the former is more traditional and the latter less so, both uses are of equal importance and are, in actuality, inseparable strategies; for through storytelling, students communicate to learn and learn to communicate.

STORYTELLING AND CULTURE

Storytelling enables students to interact with culture (past and present) through narrative, which is the major means by which children make sense of the world around them (Moffett, 1983, p. 49). As such, storytelling is a natural way for students to explore the historical past, the belief systems of varied societies, and diverse factual information as well. A story I tell, an adaptation of a ghost story originally written by Ambrose Bierce (1983), is an example. It is called "A Cold Night," the night in question being January 1, 1863.

The scene is a broad, frozen, cadaver-strewn plain spanning the Stones River near Murfreesboro, Tennessee, the aftermath of one of the Civil War's bloodiest days of fighting. For the survivors, the fight for survival continues throughout the night as the men contend with bitter cold temperatures and the persistent fear that they might be killed during the next day's fighting. In the midst of this numbing carnage, a simple act of kindness and respect is acknowledged in a rather eerie fashion.

> Late in 1862, the Union forces were divided into three armies. The Army of the Cumberland, 45,000 strong, under the command of Major General William S. Rosecrans, was situated just south of Nashville, Tennessee. The general's main objective was to march on Chattanooga and take that city, which served as a major railroad supply hub for the Confederacy.
>
> Standing between Rosecrans and Chattanooga was General Braxton Bragg and 38,000 seasoned Confederate veterans, encamped just north and west of Murfreesboro, all up and down the Stones River.
>
> The battle of Stones River (Murfreesboro, if you favor the Confederate cause) began on December 31, 1862. Rosecrans's men had marched from the North and West. Bragg and his troops defended from the South and East. The strategy favored by both armies was

identical, "Hold with the right line of forces, attack with the left line." Had both plans been carried out simultaneously, the armies would have swung around like a huge revolving door. But as was typical of most of the early battles in the Civil War, the Confederates struck first and drove the Union troops back and in on themselves so that, by day's end, the Union position appeared to be like a giant jackknife with the blade partially exposed.

Perhaps as a result of the confusion, the Confederates were unable to drive the Union forces from the field. Still and all, the fighting had been fierce. The volleys of musket fire alone had been so loud that soldiers on both sides of the line had plucked cotton bolls right from the plants and stuffed them in their ears to stave off the awful noise.

Now, for some unexplained reason, Bragg failed to capitalize on his victory that first day. His army sat idle on January 1 and the morning of January 2; but he took up the fight again on the afternoon of the 2nd, and he was repelled that day by savage cannon fire. Fifty-eight Union cannons that were lined up in a row tore Bragg's line to shreds, one of the few instances during the war when cannon fire played a significant role in turning the tide of a battle.

Two days later, Bragg had retreated to Tullahoma, Tennessee, 36 miles to the south, and Rosecrans walked into Murfreesboro. The Battle of Stones River was over.

Who won the battle? Of what significance was it? No one can say! Nothing of any military consequence had been gained. Rosecrans claimed victory, of course, for Bragg had retreated from the field of battle. But at what cost?

Both armies would be immobilized for several months. And it is an axiom of war that if you cannot fight, you cannot win. And the casualties? The dead and the wounded? 13,000 for the Union, 10,000 for the Confederates, well over a quarter of the strength of both armies.

Now, one of the Union soldiers still alive at the end of the first day's fighting was Ambrose Bierce, the noted Civil War chronicler and a captain in an Indiana regiment. On that first day, Bierce and his companions had taken refuge behind a railroad embankment that served as a breastwork staving off the repeated charges of Confederate infantry. Before the embankment lay the dead of both armies piled two or three deep. Behind the embankment, the ground was flat, broad, open, and strewn with sizable boulders. And next to nearly every boulder were Union dead, soldiers who had been dragged out of the way during the battle.

When the fighting had subsided late, the heat of the fighting was replaced with a piercing cold, a crystal clear night despite clouds of gunsmoke created earlier in the day, a night frozen and unyielding.

Among the dead lay one whom no one seemed to know, a sergeant, flat on his back, his limbs outstretched, rigid as steel. He had died on the spot where he lay . . . or so it seemed.

He had been shot squarely in the center of the forehead with a miniball. One of the Union surgeons (perhaps out of idle curiosity, perhaps to amuse the still-living soldiers gathered nearby) pressed a probe clean through the sergeant's head until it struck dirt at the base of the skull.

The night had grown so frigid that frost had formed on the grass around the sergeant, on his ashen face, his hair, and his beard. Some Christian soul had covered him with a blanket; but as the night turned colder and unrelenting, a companion of Bierce's approached the body, took hold of that blanket and said in a solemn voice, "Please forgive me, sir. But I fear I'll be needing this more than you tonight." He took the blanket and then both he and Bierce wrapped themselves in it and suffered through the night.

That night, every man lay still and silent. Pickets had been posted well out in front of the railroad embankment. These soldiers were permitted to move to insure the security of the army, but movement by all others was prohibited. Conversation was strictly forbidden. There was to be no movement, no sound, no light, no heat. To have lit even a match would have been a grave offense. Stamping horses, moaning wounded, anything that made noise had been sent well to the rear. All the living suffered the bitter cold in silence, contemplating the friends they had lost that day or perhaps the imminence of their own demise on the morrow. I tell you this to suggest that this was not a scene for a ghastly (or perhaps, I should say a ghostly) practical joke.

When the dawn broke, it broke clear. "It's likely we shall have a warm day of it; the fighting and all," remarked Bierce's companion. "I'd best return the poor devil's blanket."

He rose and approached the sergeant's body. It was in the same place but not in the same attitude. Instead of lying on its back, it was on its side, the chin tucked to its collarbone, its knees pulled up tight to its chest. The collar of its coat was turned upward, its shoulders hunched, its head retracted into the collar. And its hands were thrust to the wrist into its coat. This was the posture of someone who had died of extreme cold, not a gunshot wound. And yet there was the unmistakable evidence, the bullet hole through the head. But within arm's reach of that young dead sergeant, etched in the frost in the grass were written the words, "You are forgiven."

The story is captivating; it never fails to appeal to audiences in upper elementary school through high school. Beyond being entertaining, however, the tale is also edifying. Woven into the fabric of the text are facts about the battle: the dates, the setting, the nature of the fighting that took place. Through the story, students encounter the commanders of both armies and their battle plans. Terms such as *picket* and *breastwork* are introduced; their meanings clarified by means of context. Embedded in the story are elements that are sure to rouse discussion and clarify values: the merit of war, the dehumanization of combatants, the necessity for maintaining humane behavior in an uncivilized world. Introducing children to history through stories such as "A Cold Night" involves emotional as well as intellectual response on their part and thus transforms the study of history from the memorizing of facts or analyzing of irrelevant abstractions to relating past events to one's own life today, what Levstik (1986) refers to as discovering the emotional truth.

STORYTELLING AND LITERACY

Although acculturation is important, most teachers of young children believe that literacy is more critical for them to teach because it is their immediate responsibility. What we know about a preschooler's oral language growth suggests that storytelling in the classroom is a vital strategy in helping children master print as efficiently as they earlier mastered the oral language.

Compared with children's success rate in learning to communicate orally, their success in learning to read and write is dismal. Nearly all children are in control of oral language by age 5 (Bryen, 1982); yet many of these same children fail to learn to read and write after 12 years of formal education, a curious anomaly given the fact that a child's capacity for mastering both oral and print discourse is basically the same. The implication for classroom instruction is obvious; success follows when students are encouraged to employ the same strategies they used in developing oral language skills. Moreover, it makes sense to use children's knowledge to help them function with print. It is in this context that storytelling becomes a vehicle for teaching and learning.

Language Acquisition

When preschoolers learn to speak, *they are in complete control of the process.* They determine what, when, and how long to learn. Language acquisition is *effortless and enjoyable* because nobody places arbitrary conditions on the children, as is often the case in schools. *Meaning is the single focus of the children's attention.* Gradually, by selective trial and error, they determine "how to mean," that is, what formulations are most effective to get across their meaning. The result is that they come to employ the basic language used by individuals around them (typically, the child's family members), who serve as models of the mature formulations, provide feedback, and support the children in their efforts to improve their language skills. They do so by conversing with the children. In short, children learn to listen and speak by actually listening and speaking. Actual practice is performance. Language development is therefore holistic, undertaken as part of real events.

Although practice is nonstop, it is risk-free. Children are rarely penalized for experimenting, even when their utterances are only a rough approximation of mature language. From practice, children learn that listening and speaking are, themselves, active and "experimental" processes wherein they use their background knowledge to *predict and create* the oral text that they hear or speak (Lindfors, 1980; Goodman, Smith, Meredith, & Goodman, 1987).

Implications For Classroom Instruction

From this description it is possible to generate guidelines for improving classroom instruction in speaking, listening, reading, and writing:

1. Oral language must serve as the basis for all reading and writing.
2. Reading and writing must always be enjoyable.
3. Activities must be valid, holistic, and realistic.
4. Real communication must be emphasized, not concocted, meaningless activities focusing on isolated language elements abstracted from context, and completed solely as an academic exercise.
5. Because of the importance of background knowledge, children must be given an opportunity to engage in many firsthand experiences and then encouraged to employ their knowledge when reading and writing.
6. Teachers should serve as models of the very behavior they expect the students to emulate, by using all modes of communication with their students.

In short, teachers must structure classroom activities so that they involve listening, speaking, reading, and writing in a meaningful context. In this way, students will be encouraged to practice reading and writing in the same way they developed oral language expertise.

MODEL LESSON PLANS

In the appendix to this chapter are three model lesson plans that feature storytelling. Each plan contains three parts: purpose, logistics, and procedure. In each case, student enjoyment is enhanced by the teacher who chooses stories that both teacher and children personally enjoy.

Teaching objectives vary according to age. In preschool through the second grade, the children learn that stories reside in the minds of humans or in books. They learn to predict what will happen next and to read along when parts of stories are repeated. They also develop higher level thinking skills as they discuss art in published books and illustrate their own Big Books.

In the second through fourth grades, the children develop a functional understanding of story structure and become acquainted with the notion that folktales naturally change from one telling to another. They retell and write stories while improving their ability to communicate and work cooperatively with others.

The concept of "communicating to learn while learning to communicate" is most readily observable in the plan for the 5th through 12th grades. As the children recall important facts and learn new words via context clues, they clarify their understanding, engage in meaningful discussion, and improve their ability to discuss. In the process, they demonstrate their understanding of the literal elements of a story, improve their ability to read maps and develop higher level thinking skills while improving their ability to speak, read, write, and create works of art.

In the third part of each plan, the content and sequence of storytelling activities is outlined. The teacher either tells or reads stories, followed by one of several related activities. In preschool through the 2nd grade, the children analyze illustrations and produce their own pictures for the class book. In the 2nd through 4th grades, the groups write and edit their own stories. And in the 5th through 12th grades, the children report on and discuss their own research and tell stories.

Sometimes, the original stories themselves are changed to meet the particular demands of the lesson. In the preschool through first grades, Wolkstein's (1977) original story, *The Visit,* is altered to make the Big Book version more predictable. The revised text reads:

One morning, a little ant left home. She stepped over a pebble, and on she went. She walked over a stone, step by step, and on she went. She walked over a rock, step by step by step, and on she went. She walked over a boulder, step by step by step by step. And there on the other side of the boulder, she met her friend.

"Hello," he said.

"Oh, hello," she said.

They hugged, and kissed, and talked for hours and hours. Then it was time for the little ant to go home.

"Good bye," he said.

"Good bye," she said.

Then the little ant walked back over the boulder, step by step by step by step, and on she went. She walked back over the rock, step by step by step, and on she went. She walked back over the stone, step by step, and on she went. She stepped back over the pebble, and got back home that night and went to sleep.

The class then makes a Big Book as a group. (To make the Big Book itself the teacher uses railroad board [cut to 19″ × 25″] for the covers, oak tag [cut to 18″ × 24″] for the pages, and binder rings for the binding to hold the book together.) The revised text is recorded in the Big Book so that the print is large enough to be seen by the entire class. The teacher leaves sufficient space on each page for the children's illustrations.

For the 2nd through 4th grades, several published variants of the turnip story can serve as models for the flannel board version: Domanska (1969); Parkinson (1986); Tolstoi (1968). A simplified variant follows:

Once a turnip grew and grew until it was enormous. The farmer who grew the turnip tried to pull it out of the ground. But as hard as he tried, the turnip wouldn't come up. He called to his wife. Together they tried to pull up the turnip. But it wouldn't come out of the ground. Next, the dog and then the cat tried to help. But no matter how hard the farmer and his wife, their dog, and their cat tried to get the turnip out of the ground, they couldn't pull it up. Then a tiny mouse came to help. Together, the farmer, his wife, the dog, the cat, and the mouse pulled and pulled. At last, the turnip popped out of the ground. That night for dinner they all ate the turnip, and the mouse ate the biggest piece.

For the 5th through 12th grades, a map of troop movements during the Battle of Stones River, several accounts of the battle, and the Davis text are available through the National Park Service or through local libraries or bookstores (Catton, 1960; Davis, 1982; Mitchell, 1955).

Tying Theory to Practice

All three lessons employ oral language activity as a lead-in to print activities. Students listen to the teacher recite, tell, or read various works to begin each lesson, some folklore, others not. In all cases, the print activity flows naturally from the oral language; listening, speaking, reading, and writing become integrated experiences always involving whole, meaningful texts. Attention in each activity is on meaning. Because reading and writing are enjoyable experiences for all, motivating students to read and write is easy.

The rewards are multifaceted. Teachers serve as models for student behavior and augment the children's background experience, in particular their store of knowledge about narrative structure and the history of the Civil War. Students use that background knowledge to predict and create text. Because the teacher provides a basic story framework, the pupils find prediction and creation relatively easy. For example, the vegetable-problem-solution story frame makes it easy for children to create a story. As a result, the students are rarely reluctant to tell a story and are rarely heard to mutter "What should I write about?"

STORYTELLING VERSUS READING ALOUD

Although storytelling is a versatile medium of instruction, teachers are sometimes reluctant to tell stories. They may be satisfied simply to read stories aloud to children because reading aloud is a proven teaching tool, particularly when literacy training is an issue (McCormick, 1977). They also say that without question, storytelling is a skill more difficult to develop than is reading aloud. It involves more risk taking by the storyteller, who may forget what to say or may deliver a story in a stumbling, rambling, disjointed, or otherwise embarrassing manner. With no text to fall back on, with no book to hide behind, storytellers expose something of their innermost personalities through the stories they choose to tell and by their unique styles of delivery. They therefore run the risk of personal rejection every time they perform.

With so much at stake, then, why tell stories rather than read them aloud? The answer is simple: storytelling is a more powerful, creative art form. It also has its own rewards. True, storytelling is a more risky endeavor than reading aloud, but the perceived weakness can also be viewed as a strength. No book obstructs the line of communication between teller and audience, no illustrations impede the audience's ability to concoct images along with the teller, no text limits the teller's ability to alter and personalize the telling to accommodate the audience. The audience is therefore more actively engaged in creating the story than is an audience listening to someone reading aloud. The teller and audience co-create the story from moment to moment in a more direct, personal, and creative way than can be expected in oral readings. The result is that storytelling is more powerful and satisfying for audience and teller alike. Greater risks by teachers result in greater gains by students.

LEARNING TO TELL STORIES

For many adults the greatest impediment to learning to tell stories appears to be the fear of forgetting. Teachers can minimize perceived risks in telling stories in several ways: first, by avoiding word-for-word memorizing; second, by selecting and preparing stories carefully.

An easy way to avoid memorizing is to choose stories with which storytellers are familiar, stories they have read aloud so frequently that they can simply put the book down and tell the story in their own words. No need to worry about using the original words or phrases of the author. Variation is a natural part of storytelling.

Prospective storytellers can also avoid memorizing by telling stories from their own past experiences or those of close acquaintances. "Family stories" are easy to tell because the teller is very familiar with the details: the characters, settings, and events that constitute the plot. All that the storyteller need do is arrange the details into a viable and appealing story format and sequence. (See texts specializing in this type of storytelling: Pellowski, 1987; Zeitlin, Kotkin, & Baker, 1982.)

Storytellers can also tell stories that are so logical that memorizing is not necessary. "The Ant's Visit" and "The Enormous Turnip" are examples. The little ant's trip to visit a friend follows the natural order of a trip anyone might make: leaving home in the morning and returning at night, exchanging common greetings with those she meets. And for an ant, the larger the obstacle to cross, the more steps it would take to traverse the obstacle. Similarly, the problem and solution in the turnip story are simple. The size of the characters progresses from large to small, and the repetitive nature of the scenes is easy to recall. These are stories that most storytellers need not memorize.

Many also find that, beyond selection, thorough preparation bolsters confidence. The more they practice the story, the more familiar it becomes and the more confident they become.

But practicing should be done *out loud*. It is not enough to practice by reading silently or listening to a recording of the story, although this is a good way to begin. Storytellers introduce themselves to the essential elements of the story (characters, setting, plot problem, climax, and ending)

Figure 1.1 A teacher tells a story

and create mental images of those elements as they read. They put themselves inside the story as it happens and let the story come to life in their minds. At some point, they put the original source aside and start practicing the story *out loud*. As they tell and retell the story, they will find gaps and glitches in the telling. They rethink segments that cause problems and try out alternative solutions until all the problems are solved. Gradually, the retellings become more fluid.

At some point, they feel sufficiently confident with the flow of the story to take it before an audience. Continued practice in private and before live audiences helps them polish their performance.

APPENDIX: ORGANIZING A STORY SESSION

Preschool Through First Grade

A. Purpose

1. Enjoyment

2. Develop/reinforce child's sense of story and concepts about print.

B. Logistics

1. Teacher modeling (Teacher selects stories that he/she enjoys).

2. Teacher tells story, introduces Big Book, reads aloud from text.

3. Develop/reinforce child's ability to predict upcoming text.

3. Teacher encourages children to participate as he/she tells "The Ant's Visit" and reads the Big Book.

4. Develop ability to think analytically, synthetically, evaluatively.

4. Children analyze an illustrated book; then they illustrate Big Book text with guidance from teacher.

    C. Procedure

1. Teacher recites "Invitation" (Silverstein, 1974).
2. Teacher tells "The Ant's Visit" (adapted from *The Visit* by Wolkstein [1977]) and encourages children to participate in the telling by speaking the predictable parts of the story.
3. Teacher reads Big Book version of "The Ant's Visit"; encourages children to read aloud the predictable parts.
4. Teacher reads *The Visit* (Wolkstein).
5. The class discusses illustrations: Why is it easy to see the illustrations? What shapes were used to create the ants? How can you tell one ant from the other? When the ant left/returned home, in what direction was she headed?
6. Extension Activities:

    a. Children reread Big Book, *The Visit.*
    b. Children illustrate the Big Book in teams of two. Each team illustrates one page, front and back, after class discussion: What medium shall we use? What color should the ants be? How can we tell the ants apart? Which is bigger: the boulder or pebble? the boulder or stone? the boulder or rock? the rock or stone? In what direction shall the ant go when she leaves/returns home?

Grades 2 Through 4

A. Purpose

1. Enjoyment

2. Develop child's sense of story and ability to communicate orally and in writing to peers.

3. Reinforce child's ability to think

B. Logistics

1. Teacher modeling (teacher selects stories that he/she enjoys).

2. Children listen to and retell the turnip story; write and self-edit their own vegetable story.

3. Children construct text and illus-

analytically, synthetically, evaluatively.

4. Develop child's ability to engage in cooperative learning.

trations following the original structure of the turnip story: compare and contrast versions of the turnip story.

4. Children write and edit in teams of two or three.

C. Procedure

1. Teacher recites "Invitation" (Silverstein, 1974).
2. Teacher tells "The Great Big Enormous Turnip" using a flannel board.
3. Several children volunteer to retell the turnip story using the flannel board. After each retelling the teacher encourages the class to identify similarities and differences between the retold versions, reinforces the notion that variation is natural and normal.
4. Extension Activities:

   a. Pupils name some vegetables, then select one vegetable from board list. Brainstorm potential "problems" for that vegetable; list on the chalkboard. Recall solution to the problem in the turnip story. Brainstorm potential solutions for one chalkboard problem; list them.
   b. Teacher directs pupils to write and illustrate vegetable stories in teams of two or three students. Tell them to choose a vegetable, a problem, and a solution before writing and illustrating. Encourage/support revision and editing.

Grades 5 Through 12

A. Purpose

1. Enjoyment

2. Reinforce students' ability to engage in discussion.
3. Reinforce students' ability to recall significant detail.
4. Develop students' vocabulary.

5. Develop students' understanding of the value of war.

B. Logistics

1. Teacher modeling (teacher selects stories that he/she enjoys.
2. Teacher directs discussion of story.
3. Teacher asks students to recall salient facts about the battle.
4. Students determine meaning of terms like "breastwork" and "picket" from context.
5. Students discuss the effect of war on humans.

6. Reinforce students' map-reading skill.

6. Students locate the site of the story on troop movement maps of the battle.

7. Develop students' ability to think analytically, synthetically, evaluatively.

7. Students report on significant war issues, tell a Civil War tale, create artistic battle scenes, write a Civil War alphabet book.

C. Procedure

1. Students write for information about the battle (National Park Service, Stones River National Battlefield, Rt. 10, Box 495, Old Nashville Hwy., Murfreesboro, TN 37130).
2. Teacher tells "A Cold Night" (Roney, adapted from "A Cold Night" by Bierce [1983]).
3. Follow-up discussion:

   a. Recall battle facts: when/where it took place, how long it lasted, size of armies, number of casualties.
   b. Determine from context what "breastwork" and "picket" mean.
   c. Recall facts about the ghostly incident: where it took place, who was involved, any unusual behavior.
   d. Discuss implied personalities of Bierce, the surgeon, Bierce's companion; the effect the war had on them.
   e. Discuss the pros/cons of war.

4. Using troop movement maps of the battle, have students locate where the ghostly incident likely took place.
5. Extension Activities:

   a. From various accounts of the battle, report on who won the battle, its significance, the reasons Bragg chose not to attack on January 1.
   b. Students learn to tell stories from *The Civil War, Strange and Fascinating Facts* (Davis, 1982).
   c. Students create dioramas/drawings of scenes from the story.
   d. Students write and illustrate a Civil War alphabet book.

REFERENCES

Bierce, A. G. (1983). A cold night. In E. F. Bleiler (Ed.), *A treasury of Victorian ghost stories* (pp. 311–312). New York: Scribner's.

Bryen, D. N. (1982). *Inquiries into child language*. Boston: Allyn & Bacon.

Catton, B. (1960). *The American Heritage short history of the Civil War* (pp. 116–118). New York: Dell.

Davis, B. (1982). *The Civil War, strange and fascinating facts.* Lehigh, PA: Fairfax.

Domanska, J. (1969). *The turnip.* New York: Macmillan.

Goodman, K. (1986). *What's whole in whole language.* Portsmouth, NH: Heinemann Educational Books.

Goodman, K. S., Smith, E. B., Meredith, R., & Goodman, Y. M. (1987). *Language and thinking in school.* New York: Richard C. Owen Publishers.

Levstik, L. S. (1986). Teaching history: A definitional and developmental dilemma. In V. A. Atwood (Ed.), *Elementary school social studies: Research as a guide to practice* (Bulletin No. 79, pp. 68–84). Washington, DC: National Council for the Social Studies.

Lindfors, J. W. (1980). *Children's language and language learning.* Englewood Cliffs, NJ: Prentice Hall.

McCormick, S. (1977). Should you read aloud to your children? *Language Arts, 54,* 139–143.

Mitchell, J. B. (1955). *Decisive battles of the Civil War.* Greenwich, CT: Fawcett.

Moffett, J. (1983). *Teaching the universe of discourse.* Boston: Houghton Mifflin.

Parkinson, K. (1986). *The enormous turnip.* Chicago: Whitman.

Pellowski, A. (1987). *The family storytelling handbook.* New York: Macmillan.

Silverstein, S. (1974). *Where the sidewalk ends.* New York: Harper & Row.

Tolstoi, A. (1968). *The great big enormous turnip.* New York: Franklin Watts.

Wolkstein, D. (1977). *The visit.* New York: Knopf.

Zeitlin, S. J., Kotkin, A. J., & Baker, H. C. (1982). *A celebration of American family folklore.* New York: Pantheon.

TRY THIS

To help your class understand what is meant by the term *folklore*, play a game. Place a tape recorder in a central location where it will pick up everything that is said. Then arrange a group of children in a circle and tell them that they are going to play the "folklore" game. Your class is now ready to play.

Begin by telling a joke or story to one child. Make sure that no one else hears what you say but that your message is picked up by the tape recorder. Ask the first child to whisper the same story to the next child. One after another then listens to the tale as a player whispers and passes the story or joke along to some one else.

After the last person repeats the story to the whole group, replay the first version and discuss why the two stories differ. Take time to discuss a number of possibilities. When everyone has selected the

Figure 1.2   Children passing a whispered message while
playing the folklore game

most likely reasons, replay the retellings and ask each storyteller why he or she changed the story.

Finally, ask for a definition of folklore and say that, like the game, it is always oral; a person tells a story. The same story moves by word of mouth and from one person to another, gradually changing.

—*G.B.*

CHAPTER 2

 ## CELEBRATION OF FOLKLORE

Bette Bosma

Although children already know many family stories and are interested in learning more, they may know less about the community in which they live. They may want to learn tales about their communities, about their families in the communities, and about themselves. Their teachers can use the stories to open a window on teaching opportunity, to show their charges how to collect and record tales, to organize stories in storytelling and creative writing sessions, and finally, to celebrate family and community history.

In the next chapter Bette Bosma, author of the popular book *Fairy Tales, Fables, Legends, and Myths,* describes ways teachers can encourage children to do all of these things: to collect, share, and celebrate family and community stories. Included also are ideas for capitalizing on local folklore, for recording stories, and for creating local folklore books.

You are Invited

Celebration of Folklore
Where: Seymour School north building library
When: Thursday, June 1 11:00 ~ 11:45

Heirlooms . . . Historical Events . . . Sayings and Verses . . . Traditions. These colorful signs and the friendly faces of the fifth-grade hosts and hostesses welcomed parents, schoolmates, and other guests to a festive event completely planned by the children in Pam Jackson's fifth-grade class at Seymour Christian School, Grand Rapids, Michigan. The children stood around a number of displays and explained what they collected and why it was part of folklore.

Jump-rope and handclap songs, foot-chants, and family sayings were attractively posted at the Sayings and Verses section of the library. Teachers, parents, and researchers listened to tapes the children had made and watched girls performing handclap songs such as:

Kiss, kiss, kiss
I don't wanta go to school
No more, more, more
There's a big fat teacher
At the door, door, door
They'll hand you by the collar
And make you pay a dollar
I don't wanta go to school
No more, more, more.

A boy explained Murphy's Law with a homey example:

When you eat a peanut-butter-and-jelly sandwich in the kitchen and it falls on the tile floor, it lands right side up. When you eat it in the living room, where your mom told you not to go, it lands sticky side down, and you never get the stain out of the rug.

The Traditions corner featured fifth graders dressed up like a family group: grandfather, grandmother, parents, teenager, young boys, and toddler girl. They pantomimed a family gathering, complete with posing for a photo with grandma in a rocking chair. Viewers read accounts of family holiday traditions and saw memorabilia such as a delicately embroidered tooth-fairy pillow, while listening to music that matched the tradition. The children answered questions with the self-assurance that comes from knowing their topic well.

A boy dressed in his grandfather's army uniform introduced us to the Heirloom display. The collection included old photos, family Bibles, art objects, dolls, and handmade articles. Listening to the parents' animated conversations made it clear that when they saw the collection they recalled many memories. Each child told a story about an heirloom or told listeners how he/she had tracked down the original ownership.

Children in the Historical Events group proudly told of adventures their grandfathers had had in World War II, or their fathers in Vietnam. They showed medals and souvenirs. They also told grandparents' memories of the biggest snowstorm and other natural events, as well as immigration stories. The written stories were displayed, but each child was eager to share orally. The celebration, the finale of a unit on folklore collecting planned by Pam Jackson, the fifth-grade teacher, and myself, the recorder-researcher, included seven whole class lessons during reading/language arts time, self-directed small-group work as needed, and children working independently outside of class.

BACKGROUND FOR THE STUDY

In order to stimulate children to become interested in folklore, the teacher first developed an understanding of this cultural phenomenon. The term *folklore* was coined by William Thoms in 1846 to designate "the loving study of manners, customs, observances, superstitions, ballads, proverbs, etc. of the olden time" (Jackson, McCulaloh, & Weigle, 1984, p. 5).

A definition by B. A. Botkin (1938) sets the perimeters of folklore:

> Folklore is a body of traditional belief, custom and expression, handed down largely by word of mouth and circulating chiefly *outside of commercial and academic means of communication and instruction*. Every group bound together by common interests and purposes, whether educated or uneducated, rural or urban, possesses a body of traditions which may be called its folklore. Into these traditions enter many elements, individual, popular, and even "literary," but all are absorbed and assimilated through repetition and variation into a pattern which has value and continuity for the group as a whole. (Jackson et al., 1984, p. 4)

Folklore differs from oral history in that it refers to a personal moment: a memory crystallized and preserved to become a part of a family tradition. Folklore springs up whenever families gather together to talk, celebrate, or plan. It can begin with any generation or any happening and becomes lore when it is repeated and receives a place in the family tradition. For example, the coming of the tooth fairy is common folklore within many families. Some families will follow the tradition of preceding generations, and others begin tradition with today's family. Family folklore "is its creative expression of a common past" (Zeitlin, Kotkin, & Baker 1982, p. 9), and includes artifacts such as objects produced by household artisans, needlework, photographs, and scrapbooks.

Interest in Folklore

The wide interest in family folklore is apparent in several ways. A family folklore tent, erected at the Festival of American Folklife on the National Mall for the first time in 1974, was visited by many people who stayed to relate their family stories to the folklorists there. The American Folklore Society celebrated its centennial in 1988 and 1989. Various folklore and ethnomusicological journals and newsletters published by American scholarly organizations, educational institutions, interest groups, and commercial organizations show increased readership. *The Children's Folklore Review* is published three times a year by the Children's Folklore Section of the American Folklore Society. A complete list of these publications can be received free of charge from the Library of Congress Archive of Folk Culture, Washington, DC.

Children Collecting Lore

Engaging children in collecting folklore promotes an appreciation for family and tradition. It heightens their awareness of how life about them takes shape and offers recognition of their own contribution to such culture. Other reasons for encouraging this study relate directly to language arts:

1. Children can engage in social interaction with peers as well as immediate and extended family.
2. Stories underscore the importance of language as communication.
3. Children begin to play with language, in their riddles and word games.
4. They learn to construct categories and see relationships between their experiences and those of other families.
5. They have a real purpose for writing.

FOLKLORE COLLECTING

The fifth graders began their study with rope-jumping rhymes, a universal folklore experience which is most appropriate as a springtime activity. Miss Jackson posted a newspaper article on rope jumping that featured Francelia Butler's (1989) new book *Skipping Around the World: The Ritual Nature of Folk Rhymes.* The day she started the unit, the teacher came into the classroom jumping rope to one of her childhood chants, "Cinderella." The children recognized it and responded enthusiastically. Next she showed a lively, 4-minute video, "Pop-up," produced by Bill Vits, percussionist with the Grand Rapids Symphony Orchestra, which had been shown on "Nickelodeon," a national TV program. Even though they only heard snatches of songs in the video, the children picked up the songs immediately. Then the class went outside with several jump ropes.

Later, back in the room, the group began a lively discussion about where and when they had learned the songs and compared similar rhymes. Miss Jackson informed them that this was a form of folklore. She introduced them to sayings she always heard from her mother and grandmother, such as "Your eyes are bigger than your stomach" and "Don't count your chickens before they hatch."

Identifying Lore

The next day, Miss Jackson began by saying, "Yesterday, I said that these jump-rope songs are a form of folklore. Does anyone know what folklore is, or can anyone add something to what we already know?"

They began brainstorming, and the students gave reasons why or why not something would be part of folklore. They collaborated on composing a definition and wrote in their journals, "Folklore is that which is passed down from generation to generation, from family to (different) families." The class identified and recorded all possible forms of folklore. Together they constructed a Folklore Web (Figure 2.1). Now they were ready to begin collecting.

Collecting Time

On the third day, Miss Jackson had a laminated chart on display with the six categories from the web written across the top. The poster included a sign-up sheet and note-jotting space. Now the class began discussing how they could collect their own folklore. They talked about how families are different and how some may have more folklore than others. Each child was encouraged to select one kind of lore to investigate that would fit his or her family. The students met with partners to decide on choices, and by the end most had signed their name under one of the categories.

The children's choices on the sign-up chart led to forming four working groups: The children who chose "Sayings" and "Verses" categories joined to make one group; "Historical Events" and "Legends" became another. The other two groups were labeled "Heirlooms" and "Traditions" (see Figure 2.1)

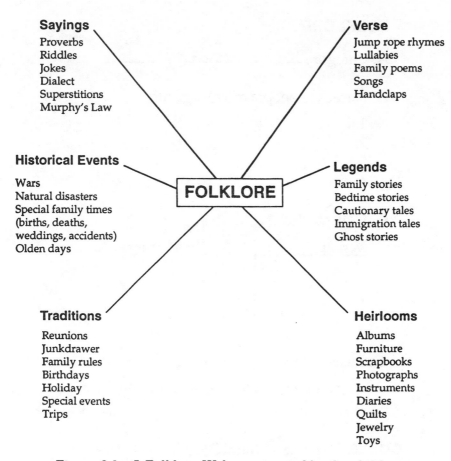

Sayings
Proverbs
Riddles
Jokes
Dialect
Superstitions
Murphy's Law

Verse
Jump rope rhymes
Lullabies
Family poems
Songs
Handclaps

Historical Events
Wars
Natural disasters
Special family times
(births, deaths,
weddings, accidents)
Olden days

FOLKLORE

Legends
Family stories
Bedtime stories
Cautionary tales
Immigration tales
Ghost stories

Traditions
Reunions
Junkdrawer
Family rules
Birthdays
Holiday
Special events
Trips

Heirlooms
Albums
Furniture
Scrapbooks
Photographs
Instruments
Diaries
Quilts
Jewelry
Toys

Figure 2.1   A Folklore Web constructed by the children

Miss Jackson encouraged the groups to begin with their own memories and to ask themselves

What do I remember?
Where did I learn it or first hear it?
Who told me?
Does it fit a particular season or special event?

Children began using the term *crystallized memory* and jotted down their ideas on a think sheet called "Collectibles & Memories" (Figure 2.2). The secretary of each group filled out the folklore category sheet (Figure 2.3).

FOLKLORE

A. Category————————————————————

B. Names of people in your group:

    1.   5.

    2.   6.

    3.   7.

    4.   8.

C. Collectables:

Verbal	Physical

D. Ideas of how to present collection:

Figure 2.2   Folklore category sheet

COLLECTIBLES & MEMORIES

Name _____

1. Memory

    –where did I learn it?

    –does it fit a season or special event?
        If so, which one?

Figure 2.3   Collectibles and memories sheet

The teacher monitored the groups and encouraged them to write out the saying, verse, story, or type of heirloom.

After collecting and recording their own memories, the young folklorists were ready to talk to parents, aunts, uncles, and grandparents. Miss Jackson held model interviewing sessions and recommended interviewing in natural settings, such as at dinner or while visiting rather than by phone. Miss Jackson passed around "Talk To" notices to help organize students' homework. She wrote "Who do I need to talk to?" in each quarter of a sheet, followed with squares for them to check off as they completed the interview. Now the pupils were ready to continue their work independently outside of class.

On day 6 the whole class discussed how to coordinate their group sharing. Will they set up a display? Will they be the display? Will they make a written collection? Each group came up with their own ideas and met with the teacher. They decided on displays and presentations in the library, complete with refreshments. A few days later they met to check with everyone to make sure they could bring in the items they had listed on their collectable list. Art period was spent making colorful signs for each group and designing invitations.

Most of the sharing at the Celebration of Folklore was through oral storying and reporting. In addition, all the children had written down their memories or information about their collectible item.

Dawn wrote about a family heirloom: "It was purchased as a gift around the 1930s. Grandma Zoodsma had used it and passed it down to her three girls in the 1960s. My mom passed it to me in 1981."

Tom shared a tradition: "A tradition my family has is a junk drawer. We keep our tape, tools, and string and whenever we need one of those things we ask Mom. She says, 'Go to the junk drawer.' My family has had a junk drawer for three generations."

The idea that folklore can begin with any generation was clearly understood by Jonathan. He brought a snake and a scorpion in glass for the heirloom collection, and wrote the following:

It started in a little souvenir shop somewhere. My grandfather bought a little rattlesnake in a glass container. He thought it was neat so he gave it to his son (my father). He passed it on to me. The scorpion was started with my generation. It was bought for me when my dad went to New York. I'm going to pass it on to my son if I have one.

BOOKS ABOUT FOLKLORE

While the children are engaged in folklore collecting, the teacher can stimulate their interest through sharing books on folklore. Some of the books listed below should be read aloud to the class, whereas others are more appropriate for independent reading and reference.

Byrd Baylor (1976) collected stories told by Arizona Native American school children. She asked children from Navajo, Hopi, Papago, Pima, Apache, Quechuan, and Cocopah tribes to tell her their favorite story told by someone in their own tribe. These stories were published in *And It is Still That Way* as a gift from those children to schoolchildren everywhere.

Jump-rope rhymes and chants from 57 countries, collected by Francelia Butler (1989) over 40 years of travel, appear in *Skipping Around the World: The Ritual Nature of Folk Rhymes*.

An American Folklore Society publication, *Folklore/Folklife*, by B. Jackson et al. (1984), was prepared for the celebration of the American Folklore Society held in both 1988 and 1989. It contains valuable information about various organizations involved in folklore preservation.

Heirloom quilts are the focus of *Patchwork Tales* by Susan Roth and Ruth Phang (1984) and *The Keeping Quilt* by Patricia Polacco (1988). Both books tell stories behind the squares of a quilt.

Alvin Schwartz was a well-known folklorist who traveled the country collecting lore. His collections delight children and offer a model for their own collecting. *A Twister of Twists, A Tangler of Tongues* (1974) includes tongue twisters from throughout the United States, with twisters in languages other than English, provided by American immigrants. *Tomfoolery* (1973) includes entertaining tricks and riddles with many of the witticisms contributed by children. Children contributed to a collection of superstitions in *Cross your Fingers, Spit in your Hat* (1974) and called these sayings "good lucks and bad lucks." Source notes and a bibliography explain the origin of many of the folk beliefs.

A group of folklorists and researchers (Steven Zeitlin, Amy Kotkin, and Holly C. Baker, 1982) present a rich collection of family reminiscences and photographs along with interpretations of forms of family lore in *A Celebration of American Family Folklore*. This book is a valuable source of information for a person planning to collect lore.

Alvin Schwartz refers to "tradition bearers," those persons who are particularly adept at recounting songs and happenings of the past. Some students may develop into tradition bearers as the result of opportunities to study folklore in the elementary school. All the children benefit from developing an awareness of the richness of their cultural heritage.

REFERENCES

Baylor, B. (1976). *And it is still that way.* New York: Scribner's.

Butler, F. (1989). *Skipping around the world: The ritual nature of folk rhymes.* Library Profession Publications.

Jackson, B., McCulaloh, J., & Weigle, M. (1984). *Folklore/folklife.* Washington DC: American Folklore Society.

Polacco, P. (1988). *The keeping quilt.* New York: Simon & Schuster.

Roth, S. L., & Phang, R. (1984). *Patchwork tales.* New York: Atheneum.

Schwartz, A. (1972). *A twister of twists, a tangler of tongues.* Illustrated by Glen Rounds. New York: Harper & Row Junior Books.

Schwartz, A. (1973). *Tomfoolery.* Illustrated by Glen Rounds. New York: Harper & Row Junior Books.

Schwartz, A. (1974). *Cross your fingers, spit in your hat.* Illustrated by Glen Rounds. New York: Harper & Row Junior Books.

Zeitlin, S. J., Kotkin, A., & Baker, H. C. (1982). *A Celebration of American family folklore.* New York: Pantheon.

TRY THIS

Help the boys and girls in your class explore their own family roots. First discuss as a group why, how, and when their ancestors came to America, where they came from, and where they went when they arrived. Also ask why they went there, how they traveled, and what kinds of adventures they had during the trip. After the children have shared a number of stories that they already know, invite them to interview a relative to learn more.

Before they talk to anyone, provide them with a guide, a form with two sets of questions. The first set should be on one side of the paper and should include:

- Where did _____ come from?
- When did _____ come?
- Why did (s)he come to America?
- Why did (s)he go to (location in the U.S.) _____?
- How did (s)he travel to that location?
- Do you know any stories about the trip?

The second set of questions, on the opposite side of the paper, should include the following:

- Where did you hear the story?
- From whom did you hear it?
- When did you hear it?

Both sets of questions should be designed to help the boys and girls discuss the topic in an organized and meaningful manner. After the interview, the children should ask the same questions of another family member to verify the story.

When everyone in the class has completed the interviews, invite them to write a story about their ancestors and how they came to America. Collect the tales in a class book or ask each child to create an individual book.

—G.B.

CHAPTER 3

❈ HELPING CHILDREN FIND THEIR PERSONAL AND COMMUNITY FOLKLORE

Sheila Fitzgerald

People often say that charity begins at home. A good deal of folklore can also be said to begin there. As Bette Bosma has already shown, many children hear stories about their parents, grandparents, aunts, uncles, and other family members. These tales, passed down from generation to generation, become family folklore that enriches children in a variety of ways at home and in school.

At home, boys and girls gain a feeling that they belong because they share a background and have similarities with others in their families. They delight in the tales they tell and take pride in tracing their own roots. Even when tales are about ne'er-do-wells and odd-balls, the stories have an important psychological value for every-one in the family, including the children.

In school, family stories can be equally important. When teach-ers tap family folklore, the children often take special pride in tell-ing and writing the stories they heard at home, enhancing their own literacy in the process.

In Chapter 3, Sheila Fitzgerald, professor of Language Arts and a former President of the National Council of Teachers of English, explores a number of writing projects that children can undertake during a unit on family folklore. The possibilities include writing stories about legendary family figures, recording family recipes, and writing letters to community members requesting favorite fam-ily recipes. All in all, this engaging material should prove a useful complement to ideas described earlier in this book.

Out of the fertile imaginations of folklorists, their astute observations of people, their ear for the delights of language, and their enjoyment of amusing or hilarious incidents, come some of the most charming books for children. Children shouldn't miss these books, which should be read to them, and which they should have many opportunities to read themselves and to read to others, outside of school as well as in school.

We stand in awe of accomplished authors, and we should. Their books represent not only their talents, but also lifetimes spent studying society's oral roots, cultivating imagination, perfecting writing skills, and pruning products. If we aren't careful, however, our admiration for published authors may intimidate us and keep us from valuing our own rich folklore—those incidents, feelings, and relationships that color our views of life and make us unique.

In her book on writing, Jacqueline Jackson (1974) draws on Lewis Carroll's poem, "The Lobster Quadrille," to point up the reluctance that we all feel about writing our own life experiences, about "joining the dance":

> Will you, won't you, will you, won't you, will you join the dance?
> Will you, won't you, will you, won't you, won't you join the dance?
> "You can really have no notion how delightful it will be
> When they take us up and throw us, with the lobsters out to sea!"
> But the snail replied "Too far, too far!" and gave a look askance—
> Said he thanked the whiting kindly, but he would not join the dance.

Writing is a scary undertaking; like the snail, we feel that we're being "thrown out to sea." We are being asked to take chances: chances that our experiences won't be appreciated or understood; chances that we won't use language in ways that people think acceptable; chances that what we find ourselves writing will be experiences we don't want to think about or remember.

But "joining the dance" of writing can be a wonderfully exciting, even if it is scary. Jackson (1974) says, "If your innards are rich and interesting, your writing is apt to be too." (p. 75). We need to look inside to see what makes us interesting. A teacher who had just taken a course that required personal writing wrote:

> I'm really into writing now. I find myself reading my work over and over and over again. I read it to myself, and I corner friends and family to listen to a few choice pieces. I'm surprised and amazed at what I'm capable of doing. I cannot remember *one* time in school—even in elementary school—when I was able to write creatively on a self-chosen topic. Writing was always for information and reaction purposes. Now I feel excited about my new found friend, writing!

This teacher probed her own folklore and the folklore of her family to find stories she enjoyed writing and sharing. From this point on she will be sure to kindle excitement for writing in the children she teaches. Children have also developed "innards that are rich and interesting" in their few short years of life, and this teacher will help them believe in themselves and their stories.

Teachers can use literature, particularly folklore, as a catalyst for generating their own personal stories and the personal stories in the lives of the children they teach. These stories will spark our awareness of the folklore that surrounds us in our families and in our communities. Yet, Harold Rosen (1981), a noted British educator, says that literature, our own and that of recognized authors, is often inaccessible to students in school:

> Literature has been treated as an activity pursued by a special select group called authors or writers and quite unlike any uses of language which pupils or ordinary mortals pursue. This in school practice has meant a disjuncture between reading and writing, even more between normal speech and literature, and between oral and written literature. Consequently, literature has been set apart from universal human uses of language. (p. 10)

What a shame! What treasures we could find in exploring the stories in our heads, the stories that we have already told to ourselves, at least in part, and the stories that have been told or read to us. It is out of this internal and external oral tradition that stories spring.

STORIES TO TELL

One teacher amazed herself when she discovered such a tale in her own innards, a story she knew well—about her one-armed, bass-strumming, foul-mouthed uncle:

MY UNCLE FUNNIER THAN A BLUE NOSED GOPHER

My uncle is one of those colorful people every family has in their tree. What makes him distinctive at first glance is that he's a one-armed bass player in a country western band. It's hard not to marvel at his talent and skill when playing a bass. He has full use of one arm and for the other he has a stub that extends just past his elbow. With that stub my uncle can accomplish about anything. Proof positive is his sustained employment after all of these years in country western bands. His talent extends beyond instrumental to vocal. He can croon a tune just as well as the big guys.

At second glance, and most outstandingly, one cannot miss the language my uncle uses that's all his own. He's cultivated, over the years, expressions and profanities that make him a rarity in a world of polish. His expressions are pure home spun. Getting passed the deluge of blankity, blank, blank blanks is not an easy task. Even after growing up around him, I must still step back, shake my ears, and adjust the tuning. Once hearing is fine tuned to be selective, he's (to borrow his own expression) "funnier than a rubber crutch." In fact, he'd say he's "funnier than a blue-nosed gopher." Unless that comment made him angry then he'd say "That's a stick in my eye" or "That's mud in the eye."

When he speaks, out of his mouth comes verbiage that is rich in a hillbilly-type flavor. Stories slip through his lips fully embellished; you can be sure he's not the author. As a child, I was embarrassed immensely by his use of language. As I grew older it disgusted me, but now I appreciate his unique, distinctive, approach to communication. He's truly one of a kind; he's my Uncle.

This teacher certainly has a story to tell here, one that has been in her mind for a long time. As time goes on, she may decide to flesh out this story a bit, telling us some of the particular words and expressions that make her "step back and shake her ears" or she may want to describe a particular time as a young girl when she was embarrassed by her uncle's language. For now, however, she has introduced us to a colorful hillbilly we're delighted to know.

Every family has at least one special person that others should meet through writing. In my family, it is my mother who is often the center of my stories:

I remember that mother could bring her five boisterous little grand-daughters to acceptable behavior simply by slapping the side of the couch where she was trying to rest, saying, "Stop that, Bruno!" Bruno was her imaginary bear who slept behind the couch. When Bruno was awakened by too much noise and bickering in our living room, he would growl and threaten to terrorize obstreperous little girls. Their improved behavior always lulled Bruno back to sleep, however, so both the grandmother and the bear got some rest.

My nieces asked their grandmother endless questions about Bruno: how she got him, if he ever came out from behind the couch, what she fed him. And they half believed the "whoppers" mom would concoct for each response. I don't remember catching any of the girls peeking behind the couch to see if there was a real Bruno back there. They may have feared for their lives—or perhaps they wanted to preserve the wonder and excitement that their grandmother could create with her temperamental bruin.

Certain holidays have special family stories associated with them. Not just one particular birthday or that Christmas when we got our first bicycle, but the enduring traditions that make family celebrations the same every year, that make Thanksgiving or Easter unique to us. Maybe it is the dime put in each birthday cake to see who will get it, or maybe it is always having to stop holiday fun to try to talk to silent Uncle Jack when he comes at noon on Christmas each year. One of my favorite descriptions of enduring family traditions at Christmas is by Dylan Thomas (1980). He starts his haunting prose poem "A Child's Christmas in Wales" this way:

> One Christmas was so much like another, in those years around the sea-town corner now and out of all sound except the distant speaking of the voices I sometimes hear a moment before sleep, that I can never remember whether it snowed for six days and six nights when I was twelve or whether it snowed for twelve days and twelve nights when I was six.
> All the Christmases roll down toward the two-tongued sea, like a cold and headlong moon bundling down the sky that was our street; and they stop at the rim of the ice-edged, fish-freezing waves, and I plunge my hands in the snow and bring out whatever I can find. In goes my hand into that wool-white bell-tongued ball of holidays resting at the rim of the carol-singing sea, and out come Mrs. Prothero and the firemen. (p. 6)

Dylan Thomas writes little about the food served at his Christmases in Wales, and much about the people who participated in preparing or enjoying the meals; but food traditions also make family memories special and offer children and teachers many opportunities for personal stories.

A TASTE FOR THE REAL THING

My younger brother Mike ate two peanut butter and jelly ribbon sandwiches for lunch every school day from grade school through high school. His weren't your ordinary peanut butter and jelly sandwiches. Each had three slices of Tastee bread with an exact amount of butter and peanut butter between each of the lower layers, and butter and Welch's grape jelly in the upper layer. All of the crusts were trimmed off carefully, and the sandwich was cut with a serrated knife into three ribbons. My mother, who doted on her youngest child, dutifully prepared Mike's sandwiches each morning—except for the day when Mike was in eighth grade and mother was so sick with the flu that she couldn't get up. I was called to the foot of her bed and given exact instructions on how to make His Highness's ribbon sandwiches. Mumbling that he was plenty old enough to make his own sandwiches, but fearing my mother's wrath if I didn't follow instructions, I went to the kitchen and prepared the sandwiches just as Mother directed, leaving Mike's lunch bag on the counter as I turned to go back to bed. Mom was feeling better when Mike came home from school that afternoon. I overheard him say to her, "What happened to my sandwiches today? They didn't taste right." I was stunned. I knew I made them just as she had told me to, just as I had watched her do hundreds of times. Perhaps I forgot some special layer of love. You wouldn't think something like that could make a noticeable taste difference.

As I wrote the incident I just described, I was smiling to myself, not just at the memory of the incident but also at the way I was writing about it; I knew I was playing fast and loose with some of the facts. Writing an incident encourages us to elaborate, reorganize the sequence, stretch the truth—plus out and out fabricate. More often than not we are influenced in our writing by all of the books that have been read to us and all of the stories we have read ourselves—not just by our memory of the incident. Glenna Sloan in *The Child as Critic* (1984) says, "Children, in fact, turn naturally to literary forms and patterns when they create stories of their own" (p. 143). I say adults do too! Children and adults who enjoy books have an intuitive sense of what makes a good story, and they shape and reshape their personal stories into "good" stories. That often means playing liberally with facts. It usually isn't authenticity we're after in writing personal stories; it is effective story making. Ian Reid (1984), an Australian educator, says:

> To integrate reading with writing . . . is to reject some assumptions behind the work of respected [authorities]. [They] apparently [suppose] that children's writing should always aim to record the authentic contours of a personal experience, one which has actually occurred before the writing itself occurs. [They] seem not to see how valid and useful it may be for young writers to fabricate a verbal experience, perhaps using a half borrowed, self-consciously "literary" language to bring into being something not felt or known until uttered. (p. 27)

At times, however, children and teachers may want to be more true to history. Like Alvin Schwartz in *When I Grew Up Long Ago*, (1978), they may make accurate reports on the lives of people they interview. Schwartz captured the "vanished world" of 1890 to 1914 by recording the remembrances of 156 older people who told him of their early family life, their holiday celebrations, the games they played, what schools were like, and so on. An elderly person told Schwartz about Iowa schools in 1900:

> There wasn't any drinking water, so usually two kids went after it. You'd go to the nearest house with a bucket. It was quite a thing to do that. It was during classes, you see, and you got out of class. But you had to be good or she wouldn't send you. Then everybody who wanted a drink would line up and use the same bucket and the same dipper. We didn't know too much about germs. (p. 60)

Tanya, a 10-year-old child, did her own interviewing of an older friend to capture the history of earlier years:

> Mrs. Pinkerton of Brooklyn [MI] thinks that schools in the 1930s were easier . . . the schools had shorter class periods that lasted only about 35 to 40 minutes. . . . And the rest [of the time] was used as a study hall . . . [for students] to catch up on their work. Classes were smaller, so consequently each [student] was given more individual help. There were more adult-type classes like sewing and cooking than academic classes. Kindergarten then was like today's pre-school. The teachers were strict [then] but expected the students' families to help them learn and to help them with their problems. Mrs. Pinkerton [thinks] that life in the 1930s was easier.

Kevin, a second grader, worked hard to get the facts right about his grandparents' arrival in America in the middle of this century:

> This is a story about my Mimi and Papa. Mimi and Papa are my grandma and grandpa. They came from Germany to America. They came on a boat. They went on a train from Germany to Genoa, Italy. They got on an old dirty boat called "Brazil." "Brazil" left Italy on August 10, 1950. The trip took 13 days. The sea was rough for a few days because of a hurricane far away. They had a tiny stateroom with two sets of bunkbeds. My Aunt Karin and Aunt Ingrid were on the boat too. The first thing they saw . . . [of] New York were the lights on the horizon. The second thing they saw was the Statue of Liberty. They did not see the Statue of Liberty up close. They saw it from far away. They were relieved that the trip was over and that they could start a new life. The End.

Patricia Case (1983) thinks there are special reasons why today's youth, like Kevin, should examine the recent past that their own grandparents and great grandparents lived:

> During the past two generations this country has progressed rapidly from a rural to an urban society. With energy and food crises becoming more evident, children are seeing that such "progress" cannot long continue. Many are beginning to question modern ways of living. They are saying, "Hey, what was done before we had supermarkets? How did people survive cold winters before natural gas and oil, before central heating?" It is valuable for each family's ways to be recorded. (p. 15)

Obviously, these biographical and historical accounts are very different from the recorded history of famous people that most of us read or wrote in the past. Cynthia Brown (1988) explains that history written from the 19th century to the end of World War II was written by trained historians, usually from upper-class backgrounds; it focused on politics and the men who participated prominently in political arenas:

> But the vast majority of people did not appear in these history books. For example, the glories of Greece were described with no mention that for every free male citizen in Greece there were at least seven slaves. What was life like for Greek slaves? We do not have testimony from them. . . . Every human event can be seen from different points of view, and every point of view is true in its limited way. (pp. 4–5)

Fleming and McGinnis (1985) explain the differences between traditional historical accounts and new ways of recording autobiographical histories:

> The new autobiographies seem more often to be written in order to gather together memories that create a pattern explaining the shape one's life has taken. Autobiographers still seem to want to explain history from a personal point of view, but instead of the recurring image of a great man looking back over his life, calmly recalling his accomplishments and his triumphs over adversity, the new autobiographies reveal more vulnerability and personal voice. (p. xiii)

We need to preserve not only personal histories but also the folklore and histories of our communities. Communities, the places we grow up, the places we live, become a part of us, who we are, what we think. They are a part of us throughout our lives, influencing our expectations and our hopes.

STUDENTS WRITING COMMUNITY FOLKLORE

Diane Orchard, a sixth-grade teacher in Lapeer, Michigan, helped her children to study themselves and their community when the class developed a book of stories, puzzles, and pictures about lumbering days a hundred years ago in their township of Attica. Paula Finkelstein's ninth-grade class at the Akiva Jewish Academy produced a booklet called "Lest We Forget: Ninth-Graders' View of the Holocaust." In the introduction to their history and their interviews with local Holocaust survivors they wrote:

> We, the ninth-grade English class of Akiva Hebrew Day School, feel it necessary to inform the world of this tragedy—to prevent it from ever happening again. We think it wise that *everyone*, Jew or Gentile, young or old, should know about this calamity,—one that many people know nothing about. This was the main reason behind our class study of the Holocaust: to learn more about this dreadful occurrence, to be aware of the signs that signal the start of such a horror, and perhaps to be able to prevent it.
>
> In this quest, we were required to define terms with some bearing on the Holocaust, as well as to write short biographies of some of the people involved. Most importantly, many of us went on interviews with survivors to profit from their first-hand experiences. We feel we have gained a great deal of knowledge and insight into their catastrophic ordeal. It is our sincere hope that you, our readers, gain as much by reading this collection of our work as we did in preparing it. In conclusion, we thank you for allowing us to express our thoughts and ideas to you.
>
> Cordially yours,
> The Ninth Grade Class of Akiva

Betty Hirschman's middle-school class created another very impressive booklet called "Art in Our Environment." The students sketched important buildings in the city of Jackson, Michigan, and then searched out the stories those buildings had to tell: how and why they were built, who used them, and how they had changed over the years. The students were so caught up in the histories they found that each page of their booklet brought to life the stone and mortar structures that made up the physical environment of their community. Their booklet was popular with parents and community leaders, as well as with the children. A copy was presented to the Jackson Historical Society—and gratefully received.

Another year, this same teacher's class was studying government and she wanted the students to read the political news in the newspaper more thoroughly. The students selected local, state, and national politicians, to whom they then wrote letters asking for pictures, descriptions of their jobs—and copies of their favorite recipes! The county sheriff sent in Jackson County Jail Goulash; Michigan's Attorney General offered Pumpkin Nut Bread; the Chief Justice of the Michigan Supreme Court contributed Spinach-Artichoke Souffle; and the President of the United States sent in his recipe for Pumpkin Pecan Pie. What could have been just a dull set of social studies reports assigned by the teacher became the children's charming mix of politics, government roles, and personalities.

My all-time favorite book of student writings about community life, however, took 100 years to mellow. In 1876, a remarkable teacher, Mrs. Lou Wilson, had a terrific idea. To honor the 100-year legacy the country was celebrating in 1876, as well as the children who lived in 1776, she asked her 39 teenage students, in School #10 in Des Moines, Iowa, to write a composition of their choice, addressing it to children who would be celebrating America's 200th birthday in 1976. The result, *1876 Centennial Offering* (1977), was such an outstanding handwritten booklet that it was sent to Washington, D.C., to be displayed during the 1876 Centennial celebration. Later the book was returned to Mrs. Wilson, and she kept it for her remaining teaching years. However, when she retired in 1917, after 56 years of teaching, Mrs. Wilson gave the book to the Iowa Historical Society. In 1976, 100 years after it was written, the museum curator dusted it off, sent it to a publisher for printing, and made it available for America's Bicentennial Celebration. What a bridge across time that book proved to be—looking back to those who came long before and dreaming far into the future about those who would build on what was started. One child, Elmer Todd, age 14, contributed his poem about life in 1876 communities:

> Our cities now are crowding fast
> With hunger, misery, want and woe,
> Poor houses multiply, alass
> And lunatic asylums too.
> The devil, you see, finds more to do
> Than he did one hundred years ago.
> The streams our fathers had to ford
> Great iron bridges o'er them go.
> And where the grizzle once was lost
> Large cities grow and flourish now,
> And daily trains that come and go
> Weren't known one hundred years ago.
> But men and women both I know
> Were true one hundred years ago.

Figure 3.1 A family photo of a shared story read at home

Another thing that's changed since then
The schoolmarms all were ugly men.
Boys of '76 would envy us I know
Could they step into our schools today,
See the pretty schoolmarms slap the lads
Just as they did one hundred years ago.
And here's to the true hearted men and boys
Who are through with lifes' battles and joys and cares
May our deeds for right and honer glow
Like their's of one hundred years ago.
                (Spelling and punctuation as originally written; unpaged)

Yes, we all have stories to tell, our own personal folklore that comes out of our private thoughts, our perceptions of what we learn from history, our families, and our communities. These sources are the real stuff of life that children's writing can be about. The books we read to children, and the books that we put into their hands for them to read themselves, will nurture children's personal stories and intuitively imprint the patterns and structures of written language on their minds.

The reading and writing opportunities offered to children, in and out of school, need to be engaging. Folklore is one important way to reach for both better reading and better writing. Jacqueline Jackson (1974) sums up for us the values of encouraging the writing and reading of personal folklore and the folklore of the community:

> I can't write well about anything I don't care about. To me the writing is second to the caring, a way of communicating the caring. Hoping you'll care, that you'll come, too. And this caring is the heart of the dance, and is the most important thing in the world. (p. 80)

REFERENCES

Anderson, G. K., & Walton, E. L. (1949). *This generation.* Glenview, IL: Scott, Foresman.

Brown, C. S. (1988). *Like it was: A complete guide to writing oral history.* New York: Teachers & Writers Collaborative.

Case, P. A. (1983). *How to write your autobiography.* Santa Barbara, CA: Woodbridge.

Fleming, M., & McGinnis, J. (1985). *Biography and autobiography in the secondary school.* Urbana, IL: National Council of Teachers of English.

Jackson, J. (1974). *Turn not pale beloved snail.* Boston: Little, Brown.

Reid, I. (1984). *The making of literature.* Sydney: Australian Association for the Teaching of English.

Rosen, H. (1981). *Neither black house nor liberty hall: English in the curriculum.* London: University of London, Institute of Education.

Schwartz, A. (1978). *When I grew up long ago.* New York: Harper & Row Junior Books.

Sloan, G. (1984). *The child as critic.* New York: Teachers College Press.

Third Ward Pupils, No. 10, Des Moines, Iowa (1977). *1876: Centennial offering.* Ames: Iowa State University Press.

Thomas, D. (1980). *A child's Christmas in Wales.* Boston: Godine.

TRY THIS

The following activities have been designed to help children explore family life through photographs. The three activities listed below have been adapted to fit the abilities and interests of children at different stages of development.

1. Ask young children, in kindergarten through second grade, to bring a photo or draw a picture of their own family group (mother, father, sisters, and brothers). Then ask them to record the name of each family member and to tell a story about one of them.
2. Invite somewhat older children, in the third through fifth grades, to collect family photos and to find out as much as they can about the people in them:

    • Who are the people in the photos?
    • Where were the photos taken?
    • When were the pictures taken?

Ask the children to prepare an album of family photos and to label each picture. Then ask them to write a story about each of the people in the photos.

3. Ask sixth through eighth grade children to interview their parents, aunts, uncles, and grandparents to find out who the unknown people in old photos were. The children can also ask questions like the following to learn more about the times in which the people lived:

    • What are the people doing?
    • What was life like when the photo was taken?
    • What did people eat and wear?
    • What was their house like? Where was it located?

After the interviews, the children can label the pictures and write stories about each of the photos. Last of all, they can arrange all of the pictures in a family album.

—*G.B.*

CHAPTER 4

❊ FINDING FOLKLORE

Margaret Read MacDonald

How can teachers help children collect folklore? Where can teachers and children go for library resources on folklore? In this engaging chapter, Dr. Margaret Read MacDonald, folklorist, librarian, and author of *The Storyteller's Sourcebook: A Subject, Title, and Motif Index to Folklore Collections for Children*, a standard reference on folklore resources, explores some of the possibilities.

Our lives and those of our students touch folklore in many ways. Since we are *the folk*, the customs that we ourselves pass on are as interesting to the folklore scholar as are those of distant and seemingly more exotic places. Students can enjoy collecting and sharing the folklore of their family, community, and friends. And they can make a valuable contribution to the folklore archives of your region by collecting and documenting properly.

FINDING FOLKLORE IN THE CLASSROOM

The teacher who wants to incorporate folklore into the classroom need look no further than the students themselves. Each student is a repository of folklore tradition. Riddles, jokes, games, songs, scary stories, and other pastimes, such as "cootie catchers," are known to every child. These are all examples of folklore items. They are passed from person to person, in this case often from child to child. These folklore items adapt themselves to the culture and the times as they migrate throughout the world and endure over centuries.

The classroom study of folklore items collected from the students themselves will demonstrate clearly the scope of folklore. Start with Motif E235.4.1, The Golden Arm, which every student knows. Read them one version, such as that in Joseph Jacobs's *English Folk and Fairy Tales*. Then ask who has heard a similar tale and let the telling flow. Compare their variants and discuss how a tale changes. Ask which tale they consider the "best," and why?

Make a classroom collection of riddles or jokes. Point out the fact that these items are, for the most part, passed around orally. Talk about ways in which jokes and riddles might change as they travel from teller to teller. Play a game of "gossip," in which the leader whispers a short story to the first of a line of listeners. Each whispers the tale to the next. The last listener retells the story out loud. Usually it has changed drastically from the leader's original telling.

To familiarize yourself with the folklore of childhood, examine these collections: *Children's Folklore: A Book of Rhymes, Games, Jokes, Stories, Secret Languages, Beliefs, and Camp Legends ...* by Simon Bronner (1988); *Children's Games in Street and Playground* by Iona and Peter Opie (1985); *Children's Riddling* by John McDowell (1979); *The Lore and Language of Schoolchildren* by Iona and Peter Opie (1987); *One Potato, Two Potato: The Folklore of American Children* by Mary and Herbert Knapp (1978); *Skipping Around the World* by Francelia Butler (1990); and *The Skit Book: 101 Skits From Kids* by Margaret Read MacDonald (1989).

For an excellent collection of Canadian children's songs, see Edith Fowke's (1985) *Sally Go Round the Sun: Three Hundred Children's Songs, Rhymes and Games*. See also indexes such as Roger D. Abrahams's (1969) *Jump Rope Rhymes: A Dictionary; Counting-Out Rhymes: A Dictionary* by Roger D. Abrahams and Lois Rankin (1980); and *A Dictionary of Superstitions* by Iona Opie and Moira Tatem (1990).

FINDING FOLKLORE IN THE HOME

To continue the study of folklore beyond the classroom, you may encourage the students to collect folklore items from their families or from the community. Your study of folklore now broadens to include family folklore and the examination of material culture. A good source to get you thinking about the varieties of family folklore is *A Celebration of American Family Folklore* by Steven J. Zeitlin, Amy J. Kotkin, and Holly Cutting Baker (1982).

The term *material culture* is used to refer to those physical objects whose creation and use are learned through the folk process. My father, for example, learned to make cedar roofing shakes from his father. Now several young men in the island community where he lives have learned shake making from him. The tradition continues. You may read several articles dealing with various items of material culture in *American Folklife* by Don Yoder (1976). The "Foxfire" series, edited by Eliot Wigginton, contains a discussion of several aspects of material culture. *Underfoot: An Everyday Guide to Exploring the American Past* by David Weitzman (1976) presents an historian's approach to examining material culture, and his *My Backyard History Book* (1975) presents some of this same material in a format designed for children.

Students may be encouraged to bring into the classroom items of material culture from their homes. Grandmother's quilt will appear, perhaps a handmade rag doll, a carved wind vane, or a woven basket. To make these items more meaningful, have your students try to elicit the stories behind the items. Does the family tell stories about the grandmother who made this quilt? Why did she make this particular quilt? A wee doll table that has survived in my family became more than just a doll table when I heard its story. It had been made by my paternal grandfather for my mother when she was a little girl. He was doing carpentry work in her home at that time. Later she grew up and married his son! She still had the doll table that her new father-in-law had made for her when she was a child.

You may also want to enter the realm of foodlore. Let the students collect family recipes. Try some of them out and sample the results! Interesting information on foodlore appears in *American Foodways* by Charles Camp (1989).

Another interesting area to explore is that of holiday customs. Each family develops its own traditions surrounding holidays. Share these customs. Each student may want to create a booklet documenting family holiday traditions. To sample holiday customs from other cultures, see *The Folklore of American Holidays* by Tristram Potter Coffin and Henig Cohen (1987) and *The Folklore of World Holidays* by Margaret Read MacDonald (1991).

FOLKLORE AS GOSSIP!

If you want to draw your students into a discussion of folklore, relate a few urban legends, a term applied to totally gross and horrifying rumors that run rampant in the United States these days. From the fifties you will recall tales of the lady with the beehive hairdo who found a nest of black widow spiders living in it. More recently we have all heard the horror story of the lady who gave her pet poodle a bath and put it in the microwave to dry.

These tales are passed along rapidly in our society. We retell them because they function for us. They deal with areas of life about which we are uneasy. Passing on these stories is a way to talk about our fears without actually mentioning them. Teens have many of these urban legends in their repertoires.

Introduce the topic by telling a few of these legends as if they were really true. When these legends are told, the teller swears that they *are* true. In fact, they are usually said to have happened to a friend of a friend. Often the teller really believes that the event did happen. After you have told an urban legend or two, someone in the class will probably volunteer "I heard of something like that that *really* happened." Let the student tell the tale, and you are on your way. After several students have shared tales, you can begin to point out similarities, talk about the function of these folklore items, and discuss them as folklore. For tons of hair-raising urban legends, see Jan Harold Brunvand's collections: *The Vanishing Hitchhiker: American Urban Legends and Their Meanings* (1981); *The Choking Doberman and Other "New" Urban Legends* (1984); *The Mexican Pet: More "New" Urban Legends and Some Old Favorites* (1986); and *Curses! Broiled Again!* (1989).

DOCUMENTING FOLKLORE

If your students are going to spend time collecting folklore, ask them to learn to document the material properly. Each item of folklore needs to be identified with the name of the informant from whom the student learned it, the date of collection, and the place of collection. Any other information, such as a short paragraph describing the uncle, say, who told this story, or the setting in which it was told, would be useful. Encourage the children and parents to put the material into a family file. It might be pulled out 50 years from now and consulted as a bit of family history. The more information included, the better. And if you decide to place your students' gatherings in a historical archive in your area, good documentation is essential. To learn more about documenting your folklore research, see Bruce Jackson's (1987) *Fieldwork,* a guide designed for folklore scholars. Two more approachable guides are Jan Harold Brunvand's (1984) *Folklore in Utah: A Guide for Collectors,* and *A Guide for Collectors of Oral Traditions and Folk Cultural Material in Pennsylvania* by MacEdward Leach and Henry Glassie (1968). The somewhat technical but very comprehensive book *The Emergence of Folklore in Everyday Life: A Fieldguide and Sourcebook,* edited by George H. Schoemaker (1990), may also prove useful.

UNDERSTANDING FOLKLORE

To increase your own understanding of folklore, read *The Dynamics of Folklore* by Barre Toelken (1979) and *The Study of American Folklore* by Jan Harold Brunvand (1988). Both authors include extensive bibliographies to help you explore specific areas further. For a revealing glimpse at one small Irish community through the eyes of a folklorist, sample *Passing the Time in Ballymenone* by Henry Glassie (1982). This book may inspire you to look at *everything* around you with renewed curiosity.

FINDING FOLKLORE IN BOOKS

Now that your students are hooked on folklore, you can expand your view into printed folklore collections. One item of folklore readily available for scrutiny from a variety of cultures is the folktale. Our scholarly libraries contain shelves of folktales collected by anthropologists and folklorists. American and British authors have drawn heavily from these sources, preparing folktale collections for children and for adult popular libraries. In preparing my *Storyteller's Sourcebook: A Subject, Title and Motif-Index to Folklore Collections for Children* (1982), I indexed 556 collections of folktales written for children. Those 556 titles were all actively in use in various school and public library children's rooms in the United States. Sorting through such a mass of material for the best titles for your own classroom is a formidable task.

When examining a collection of folktales, it is important to be aware of the processes that may have taken place in producing that volume. In many cases the collection is written by a professional author who was neither a folklorist, a member of the culture from which the tales came, or a storyteller. The author probably rewrote the tales to conform to a notion of literary style. Perhaps they were simplified for children. The language may have been limited to a certain grade level vocabulary. Descriptive detail may have been added to match the author's ideas about the culture or place of the tale. Such changes do not always improve a tale.

The source from which the author worked was probably taken down by an anthropologist during the early part of this century or the later part of the 19th century. These early texts seldom contain little more than the bare plot outlines for stories. Little mention is made of the storytellers themselves. It is unlikely that the fragmented story plots contained in these collections were collected from master storytellers. Or perhaps the collector just retold the plot, leaving out the performative aspects of the telling. Certainly these bare bones tale texts show few of the marks of a lively telling before a live audience.

Because of the nature of their sources, and the retelling styles of the authors, most of the collections published for children in the past lack the flavor and artistic quality of live storytelling events. Happily, today's folklorists record not just the tale text, but information about performance style, audience response, the context of the tellings, and the function of the tale within its culture. Examining collections that have been published in recent years can give a feel for the aesthetic quality of tale performance in another culture. To enjoy a glimpse at storytelling events in other cultures, sample books such as these: *Finding the Center: Narrative Poetry of the Zuni Indians* by Dennis Tedlock (1972); *See So That We May See: Performances and Interpretations of Traditional Tales from Tanzania* by Peter Seitel (1980); *The Magic Orange Tree and Other Haitian Tales* by Diane Wolkstein (1978); *Speak, Bird, Speak Again: Palestinian Arab Folktales* by Ibrahim Muhawi and Sharif Kanaana (1989); and *The World of Storytelling* by Anne Pellowski (1990).

SHARING FOLKLORE THROUGH STORYTELLING

One effective way to introduce students to the folktale is through storytelling. Because of the convoluted process through which stories reach print, not many of our collections lend themselves to oral telling. They have been too far removed from the teller's own words and style to retell easily. A few books have tried to keep their tellings close to the original teller's rendition. These make excellent sources for the classroom storyteller. For a list of such useful collections, see the bibliography "Collections with Texts Close to Their Oral Origins" in my *Twenty Tellable Tales: Audience Participation Folktales for the Beginning Storyteller* (1984). (For advice on storytelling, see chapter 1 of this book, by Craig Roney.)

BUILDING A BACKGROUND IN THE FOLKTALE

To understand the folktale traditions of certain countries, you may want to consult the Folktales of the World series, published by the University of Chicago Press. Each title includes a brief essay about the history of folktale research in that country and includes a selection of sample tales collected. A list of the titles in that series is given in the reference list under the name of the series editor, Richard M. Dorson. The Pantheon Fairy Tale and Folklore Library series may also prove interesting. Those collections are quite hefty and inexpensive in paperback. They are not uniformly useful for storytelling, but each volume contains so much material that it forms a good place to begin delving into the folktale base of a given culture. Both the University of Chicago and Pantheon series are published for an adult audience and are not screened for scatological material, so you may not want to hand them to elementary students without checking them over yourself. They are excellent introductory devices, however, for the teacher. You must inform yourself before you can lead your students. And the very fact that you have *this* book in your hands shows that you are eager to do just that.

CONDUCTING A FOLKTALE COMPARATIVE STUDY

Older students may find folktale comparative study fascinating. Discussion of several variants of a well-known tale such as "Cinderella" can give the students an understanding of the ways in which folktales adapt themselves to various cultures as they travel throughout the world. *World Folktales: A Scribner Resource Collection* by Atelia Clarkson and Gilbert B. Cross (1984) is an excellent tool to help you plan such units. The authors have selected a sample variant for each of 17 well-known folktales. They provide notes discussing variants of the tale and a short bibliography showing where other variants can be located. The book also includes a chapter describing a folktale unit developed for a college classroom, taught by the authors. You may also find my own storytelling collections useful for facilitating comparative tale study. *Twenty Tellable Tales* (1984), *When the Lights Go Out* (1986), and *Look Back and See* (1991b) all include notes that discuss each tale's variants and help you locate those variants in other sources.

USING FOLKTALE INDEXES

Once you decide on a tale for study, you will want to consult a folktale index to find out where you might locate other variants of your tale. If you are dealing with adult material, you should consult Stith Thompson's (1966) *Motif-Index of Folk-Literature* and *The Types of the Folktale* (1973) by Annti Aarne and Stith Thompson. These are the two indexes that folklorists throughout the world use to classify folktales. You might think of them as the "Dewey Decimal" system of the folktale. Each complete tale is assigned one "Type" number. Cinderella, for example, is Type 510. Within each tale there may be several motifs. Cinderella contains such motifs as "slipper test—H36.1" and "three-fold flight from the ball—R221." Don't worry too much about figuring all this out. Just understand that a tale may be identified by its assigned number. If the notes in a Japanese tale collection refer to a tale as Type 510, you know that the Japanese folklorist has identified this tale as a variant of Cinderella.

Motif-Indexes have been compiled for several culture areas. They are found mainly in large scholarly libraries, so in-depth research into an area may require a trip to a university library. However, the basic *Motif-Index of Folk-Literature* is available in the main library of most urban areas. If you are dealing with children's folktale collections, you are in better luck. *The Storyteller's Sourcebook: A Subject, Title, and Motif-Index to Folklore Collections for Children* (MacDonald, 1982) indexes 556 folktale collections and 425 picture books. It is available in most public library systems and in many school districts. With this tool even the novice can look up the motif number for a folktale and discover a list of variants with their sources. You can approach the index by looking up either a tale title or a subject. The subject approach is especially useful if you are trying to plan a unit around a theme. For example, if you want stories about "soap" for a certain unit, you can find them listed here. An ethnic and geographic index is also included.

Now go do it! You have here several approaches to the use of folklore in the classroom, along with enough bibliographic cues to keep you reading for a long time! I hope you and your students have great success in your adventures tracking folklore.

REFERENCES

Aarne, A., & Thompson, S. (1973). *The types of the folktale: A classification and bibliography* (Folklore Fellows Communications No. 184). Helsinki: Suomalinen Tiedeakatemia.

Abrahams, R. D. (1969). *Jump-rope rhymes: A dictionary.* Austin: University of Texas Press.

Abrahams, R. D., & Rankin, L. (1980). *Counting-out rhymes: A dictionary.* Austin: University of Texas Press.

Bronner, S. (1988). *Children's folklore: A book of rhymes, names, jokes, stories and camp legends.* Little Rock, AR: August House.

Brunvand, J. H. (1981) *The vanishing hitchhiker: American urban legends and their meanings.* New York: Norton.

Brunvand, J. H. (1984a). *The choking doberman and other "new" urban legends.* New York: Norton.

Brunvand, J. H. (1984b). *Folklore in Utah: A guide for collectors.* Salt Lake City: Utah Heritage Foundation.

Brunvand, J. H. (1986). *The Mexican pet: More "new" urban legends.* New York: Norton.

Brunvand, J. H. (1989). *Curses! Broiled again!: The hottest urban legends going.* New York: Norton.

Butler, F. (1990). *Skipping around the world.* New York: Ballantine.

Camp, J. C. (1989). *American holidays.* Little Rock, AR: August House.

Clarkson, A., & Cross, G. B. (1984). *World folktales: A Scribner resource collection.* New York: Scribner's.

Coffin, T. P., & Cohen, H. (1987). *Folklore of American holidays.* Detroit: Gale Research.

Dorson, R. M. (Series Ed.). *Folktales of the World.* Chicago: University of Chicago Press.

       Eberhard, W. (1968). *Folktales of China.*

       El Shamy, H. (1982). *Folktales of Egypt.*

       Briggs, K. (1968). *Folktales of England.*

       Beck, B. (1987). *Folktales of India.*

       O'Sullivan, S. (1968). *Folktales of Ireland.*

       Noy, D. (1969). *Folktales of Israel.*

       Paredes, A. (1987). *Folktales of Mexico.*

       Christiansen, R. (1968). *Folktales of Norway.*

Fowke, E. (1985). *Sally go round the sun: Three hundred children's songs, rhymes and games.* New York: Dover.

Glassie, H. (1982). *Passing the time in Ballymenone: Culture and history of an Ulster community.* Philadelphia: University of Pennsylvania Press.

Jacobs, J. (n.d.). *English folk and fairy tales.* New York: Putnam.

Jackson, B. (1987). *Fieldwork.* Urbana: University of Illinois Press.

Knapp, M., & Knapp, H. (1978). *One potato, two potato: The folklore of American children.* New York: Norton.

Leach, M., & Glassie, H. (1968). *A guide for collectors of oral traditions and folk cultural material in Pennsylvania.* Harrisburg: Pennsylvania Historical and Museum Commission.

MacDonald, M. R. (1982). *The storyteller's sourcebook: A subject, title, and motif index to folklore collections for children.* Detroit: Neal-Schuman/ Gale Research.

MacDonald, M. R. (1984). *Twenty tellable tales: Audience participation folktales for the beginning storyteller.* New York: Wilson.

MacDonald, M. R. (1986). *When the lights go out: Twenty scary tales to tell.* New York: Wilson.

MacDonald, M. R. (1989). *The skit book: 101 skits for kids.* Hamden, CT: Linnet/ Shoe String.

MacDonald, M. R. (1991a). *The folklore of world holidays.* Detroit: Gale Research.

MacDonald, M. R. (1991b). *Look back and see: Active tales for gentle tellers.* New York: Wilson.

McDowell, J. (1979). *Children's riddling.* Bloomington: Indiana University Press.

Muhawi, I., & Kanaana, S. (1989). *Speak, bird, speak again: Palestinian Arab folktales.* Berkeley: University of California Press.

Opie, I., & Opie, P. (1985). *Children's games in street and playground*. Oxford: Oxford University Press.

Opie, I., & Opie, P. (1987). *The lore and language of schoolchildren*. Oxford: Oxford University Press.

Opie, I., & Tatem, M. (1990). *A dictionary of superstitions*. Oxford: Oxford University Press.

Pellowski, A. (1990). *The world of storytelling: A practical guide to the origins, development and applications of storytelling*. New York: Wilson.

Schoemaker, G. H. (1990). *The emergence of folklore in everyday life: A fieldguide and sourcebook*. Bloomington, Trickster.

Seitel, P. (1980). *See so that we may see: Performances and interpretations of traditional tales from Tanzania*. Bloomington: Indiana University Press.

Tedlock, D. (1972). *Finding the center: Narrative poetry of the Zuni Indians*. Lincoln: University of Nebraska Press.

Thompson, S. (1966). *Motif-index of folk-literature*. Bloomington: Indiana University Press.

Toelken, B. (1979). *The dynamics of folklore*. Boston: Houghton Mifflin.

Weitzman, D. (1975). *My backyard history book*. Boston: Little, Brown.

Weitzman, D. (1976) *Underfoot: An everyday guide to exploring the American past*. New York: Scribner's.

Wigginton, E. (1972). *The foxfire book*. New York: Doubleday. [Other books from the Foxfire series: *Foxfire two* (1972) through *Foxfire nine* (1986).]

Wolkstein, Diane. (1978) *The magic orange tree and other Haitian folktales*. New York: Knopf.

Yoder, D. (1976). *American folklore*. Austin: University of Texas Press.

Zeitlin, S. J., Kotkin, A. J., & Baker, H. C. (1982). *A celebration of American family folklore: Tales and traditions from the Smithsonian collection*. New York: Pantheon.

TRY THIS

We all have folktales to tell, and many of these tales we tell have to do with our families. To help children appreciate that they themselves can recount family tales, stimulate them by telling one of your own. (Mine usually involves relating how my great-grandmother got her finger caught in the sewing machine.) Your story will help the children remember similar narratives. With only a little encouragement from you, they will take pleasure in sharing their tales.

As follow-up, urge the youngsters to ask their parents, grandparents, and other relatives for tales of long ago, stories about when the old folks were young. The children can retell the second round of stories at the next storytelling session.

After many children have shared family stories, point out that their tales are part of the oral tradition; that most stories begin among the folk; and that everyone, young and old, is part of the very same folk tradition. You will thereby encourage the children to become storytellers while helping them understand more about the folklore process.

Jim Cipielewski

PART II

❧ UNDERSTANDING THE FOLKLORE PROCESS INTRODUCTION

Folktales often seem surprisingly similar to each other, so much so that one is tempted to say, "Once you have heard one, you have heard them all." Many begin and end with the same phrases ("Once upon a time," and "They lived happily ever after.") Some have similar story structures (for instance, the cumulative one found in "The House that Jack Built" and "Why Mosquitoes Buzz in People's Ears," as told by Verna Aardema). Still others share story details or motifs, the smallest elements repeated in one story after another. (For instance, transformations as found in "Beauty and the Beast" and "The Frog Prince.")

But even when traditional stories are similar, they are also different from each other in a variety of ways. An example is "Cinderella." Although there are hundreds of stories about Cinderella-like characters, all of them have different tasks to complete and they receive help from a variety of magical figures: a fairy godmother, a dead fish, the "Month Brothers," to mention only a few. In the similarities and differences lie a treasure trove of teaching possibilities.

In the following chapters, Dr. Patricia J. Cianciolo, well-known authority on children's literature, Dr. Donald Haase, German scholar, and Dr. Bette Bosma, nationally known folklorist, underscore some of the ways teachers can take advantage of the likenesses and differences among fairy tales. Professor Haase examines stories that children can use as they learn to change traditional tales. Dr. Cianciolo explores how teachers can take advantage of the similarities and differences in fairy tales, first by drawing connections between stories and culture, second by recognizing and creating their own variants through pictures. Finally, Bette Bosma describes new approaches to teaching fairy tales.

CHAPTER 5

MOTIFS: MAKING FAIRY TALES OUR OWN

Yours, Mine, or Ours? Perrault, the Brothers Grimm, and the Ownership of Fairy Tales

Donald Haase

Many of us think of fairy tales, like the tales of the Brothers Grimm, as treasures from the past. And they are indeed treasures, but that does not mean that they are fixed and must be told exactly as the Brothers Grimm told them. We know from a variety of sources that folklore is always in process. We also know from Bette Bosma and Sheila Fitzgerald that we all have our own family and community folklore. Obviously, our personal and community tales are always in flux.

But should we change classical fairy tales like those recorded by the Brothers Grimm in Germany, Asbjornsen and Moe in Norway, and Joseph Jacobs in England and the Celtic countries? In this first of several chapters on changing old fairy tales, Donald Haase points out that alterations in fairy tales help make the old tales express our feelings, our experiences, and our times. In the process, the old tales once more become part of the folklore process.

THE REVERED PLACE OF FOLKLORE

In 1944 W. H. Auden decreed that Grimm's fairy tales are "among the few indispensable, common-property books upon which Western culture can be founded . . . [I]t is hardly too much to say that these tales rank next to the Bible in importance" (p. 1).

Auden was in one sense right. Like the Bible, fairy tales—especially the classic tales of Charles Perrault and the Brothers Grimm—hold a revered if not sacred place in modern Western culture. Often thought to reach back like sacred works to "times past," to some ancient, pristine age in which their original tellers spoke mythic words of revelation, folk tales and fairy tales are endowed by many readers with unassailable moral and even spiritual authenticity.

Because such tales had their genesis in an oral tradition, we are tempted to imagine their original tellers as simple folk endowed with infallible wisdom and, in some cases, divine inspiration. As a consequence of that belief, tampering with the classic texts of Perrault or the Brothers Grimm is considered by some to be tantamount to sacrilege, similar to revising the text of the Holy Scriptures. As one of my undergraduate students remarked in a journal he kept while studying fairy tales in the winter term of 1990: "I am not a deeply religious person. However, I have a vague feeling that questioning the origin of fairy tales is somehow sacrilegious." Some traditionalists even go so far as to argue that the common practice of replacing *Sneewittchen,* the Grimms' original German spelling of Snow White, with the more modern orthographical form *Schneewittchen* constitutes "monument desecration" (Bausinger, 1980, p. 46).

When classic stories are changed unacceptably, the blame is often placed on the culture industry—publishers, advertisers, merchandisers, and even pedagogues who have capitalized on the mass appeal of the traditional tales and emptied them of their original vigor and truth. Disney's Americanized and romanticized fairy-tale movies, for example, have been severely criticized for trivializing and betraying the original themes, thus enfeebling an important cultural possession (Bettelheim, 1976, p. 210). As the civilized entrepreneur and creator of the fairy tale as consumer romance (Haase, 1988), Disney is the absolute antithesis of the mythic peasant or Ice Age storyteller, from whom we have supposedly inherited this allegedly sacred possession.

While this religious or quasi-religious reverence is certainly appealing and even reassuring, it is dangerously misleading. As an antidote to it, consider two of the 24 theses offered by the German writer Wolfdietrich Schnurre in a piece he aptly entitled "Heretical Thoughts on the Treasury of Fairy Tales." In a sardonic letter to the long deceased Brothers Grimm, Schnurre (1978/1986) seeks to explain why he thinks fairy tales have lost their value for us. "The primary guilt for the decline of the fairy tale," he claims, "rests with those who [originally] made them. They forgot to impress on them the stamp of copyright" (p. 23). In this case, not the culture industry, but the folk themselves are held responsible for the fairy tale's bankruptcy. Ironically, the fairy tale's status as communal property is proposed as the very cause of its neglect and demise. It is a fairy tale, Schnurre asserts, to believe "that fairy tales are the property of the *Volk*—the people. Property is cared for. The *Volk*," he asserts, "has ruined fairy tales" (p. 23).

These statements are heretical to established views that tell us not only why folktales are still relevant but to whom they belong. However we might feel about the tales of the Brothers Grimm or Perrault, Schnurre's provocative assertions raise intriguing questions about the reception and cultural ownership of fairy tales. Who are the folk, that anonymous group we often view as the originators and owners of the fairy tale? And if the tales do not belong to the folk, then to whom do they belong? And, finally, why does the issue of ownership matter at all?

THE NATIONALISTIC VIEW OF FOLKLORE

The concept of "the folk" is a slippery one. To some, the folk are an ethnic or national group sharing common traditions, lore, and social or cultural traits. In general parlance, "the folk" are the common folk, that is, the working or peasant classes. But as the Italian folklorist Giuseppe Cocchiara (1952/1981) has suggested, the identity of the folk transcends classes and "is the expression of a certain vision of life, certain attitudes of the spirit, of thought, of culture, of custom, of civilization, which appear with their own clearly delineated characteristics" (p. 4). While Cocchiara's definition avoids the class bias of earlier definitions, Alan Dundes (1965) excises the ethnic and national emphasis by defining the folk as "*any group of people whatsoever* who share at least one common factor" (p. 2).

However, for the Grimms and many early folklorists, it was the so-called common people who best embodied a nation's folk life. It was their lore—including their folktales—that was to become the reservoir and model of national character. As the product of the German folk, the tales were thought to contain the scattered fragments of ancient Germanic myth, which—when collected—would provide the German people with a magic mirror in which they could discern and thus reassert their national identity. In this way, the Grimms' collection of folktales was conscripted into nationalistic service and became a political weapon in the Grimms' intellectual resistance to the Napoleonic occupation of their beloved Hessian homeland.

To define the folk in nationalistic terms establishes fairy tales as national property. They are either yours, or they are mine. Following—and, it must be emphasized, grossly exaggerating—the Grimms' nationalistic understanding of fairy tales, many Germans were only too ready to exercise their right of ownership by advocating the Grimms' tales as a national primer, after 1871, for the newly unified nation. In 1899, for instance, Carl Franke gave this explanation of the close link between the Grimms' tales and the education of a nation:

"To the spirit of German schoolchildren the tales have become what mother's milk is for their bodies—the first nourishment for the spirit and the imagination. How German [are] Snow White, Little Briar Rose, Little Red Cap, the seven dwarfs! Through such genuine German diet must the language and spirit of the child gradually become more and more German. . . ." (cited in Snyder, 1951/1978, p. 51)

Given the Grimms' precedent and given the need of every new state to authenticate its self-image, we can understand such remarks; just as we can understand the lamentable exploitation of the Grimms' tales under National Socialism, which points up all too clearly the dangers inherent in viewing fairy tales as the property of a single group or nation. (See Kamenetsky, 1972, 1977, 1984; Zipes, 1983a, pp. 134–69.)

But there is another, hidden danger in this nationalistic view. Ironically, the abuse of the Grimms' tales by the culture industry of National Socialism has reinforced prejudice against the Grimms' tales. So compelling was the German identification of Germanic folktales with national identity that the Grimms' stories have very often been accepted as belonging uniquely to the Germans. But instead of identifying favorable cultural traits in the tales, some readers have discerned more ambiguous characteristics. In 1939, Vincent Brun accused the Germans of perverting the fairy tale by exploiting its rude primitive instincts to educate and not to amuse children. By the end of World War II, the German fairy tale had fallen into such disrepute that during the Allied occupation of Germany fairy tales were viewed with serious suspicion and banned from the public school curriculum. Evidently, Auden's reclamation of the Grimms' tales as common property in 1944 was not universally accepted; in 1947 T. J. Leonard let loose with his infamous attack on German fairy tales, which he unequivocally condemned as relics of Germanic barbarism, and blamed for promoting German nationalism and sadistic behavior among Germans. The reverberations of such attacks on Germanic folktales and German national character can still be felt. In 1985, Siegfried Heyer published an abridged German translation of Leonard's attack, and Jörg Becker, in response, reflected on the enduring image of the "ugly German." That the alleged connection between German national character and fairy tales should occupy scholars 40 years after the war is not surprising given that Germans, as well as their former adversaries, have kept this essentially postwar issue alive.

In 1978, Louis Snyder repeated the thesis he first put forth in the 1950s that the Grimms' tales, having played a role in the development of modern German nationalism, emphasize "such social characteristics as respect for order, belief in the desirability of obedience, subservience to authority, respect for the leader and the hero, veneration of courage and the military spirit, acceptance without protest of cruelty, violence, and atrocity, fear of and hatred for the outsider, and virulent anti-Semitism" (p. 51). Readers like Snyder clearly relinquish title to the tales and deed them back to their owners. The nationalism implicit in the message is clear: these tales are yours (German), not mine (American).

Differentiating between tales belonging to different countries, and thus differentiating between the countries themselves, has become standard practice. In his study of the French folktale during the Old Regime, the historian Robert Darnton (1984) has insisted on the unique characteristics of the French folktale that distinguish it from its German counterpart. Darnton summarizes the differences in this way:

> Where the French tales tend to be realistic, earthy, bawdy, and comical, the German [tales] veer off toward the supernatural, the poetic, the exotic, and the violent. Of course, cultural differences cannot be reduced to a formula—French craftiness versus German cruelty—but the comparisons make it possible to identify the peculiar inflection that the French gave to their stories, and their way of telling stories provides clues about their way of viewing the world. (pp. 50–51)

Although Darnton tries to avoid stereotyping national character by adding a disclaimer and by referring instead to differing world views, in the final analysis his implicit notion of fairy tales as culturally defined property makes this difficult. However, he is at least aware of the danger of idealizing the national ethos. In pointing to the similarity between the tales of French peasants and those of Perrault, Darnton says that both groups of "tales communicated traits, values, attitudes, and a way of construing the world that was peculiarly French. To insist upon their Frenchness," he notes, "is not to fall into romantic rhapsodizing about national spirit, but rather to recognize the existence of distinct cultural styles, which set off the French . . . from other peoples identified at the time as German, Italian, and English" (p. 63). Perhaps it is easy for Darnton to avoid rhapsodizing because he is not French. That is, the tales he discusses are "theirs," not his.

Although the French are not immune to praising the unique nature of their national fairy tales, they seem to be less dependent on the tales for the codification of their self-image than are the Germans. France lacked—indeed, did not need—strong nationalistic voices such as those of the Brothers

Grimm, who set the German precedent for folktale worship. Moreover, because the French enjoyed a strong literary heritage, they were perhaps more likely to find models of the national ethos in their classical canon than in popular folk literature. After all, unlike the Grimms' tales, Perrault's stories are usually considered not so much examples of the folk culture as part of the elevated literary tradition of the Old Regime. Although Robert Darnton might find the French popular tale characterized by the earthy and bawdy, Paul Hazard (1947) praises Perrault's fairy tales for their expression of such typically French characteristics as logic, wit, and refined femininity (pp. 121–124). Fernand Baldensperger, not without irony, has even observed that Perrault's fairies are charming Cartesian fairies (cited in Hazard, 1947, p. 122).

The pride the French take in their tales rarely gets more impassioned than this. Perhaps this also has something to do with the influential essay on Perrault written by Sainte-Beuve in 1851, in which he stressed not only the naivete and simplicity, but also the universal appeal of the French stories (Sainte-Beuve, 1944, p. 273).

Such a view draws on another interpretation of the folk that does not rely on national or ethnic identity and consequently proposes an alternative ownership for the fairy tale. This view of the folk is informed by a universalizing tendency that completely disregards social, historical, and cultural factors. It is the view espoused in particular by psychoanalytic, archetypal, and anthroposophical-spiritualist (Waldorf school) readers of fairy tales. It is best summed up in this amazingly wrongheaded passage taken from the book *Fairy Tales and Children* by psychologist Carl-Heinz Mallet (1984):

> Fairy Tales are popular poetry, for they originated and developed among the people [the folk]. They were born in fusty spinning rooms. Simple people told them to simple people. No one else was interested in these "old wives' tales." No superior authority, whether profane or ecclesiastic, exerted any influence. Fairy tales developed outside the great world, beyond the centers of political and cultural power. They absorbed nothing from these areas, no historical events, no political facts, no cultural trends. They remained free of the moral views, behavioral standards, and manners of the various epochs. . . . Human beings *per se* are the focal point of fairy tales, and people are pretty much alike no matter when or where they have lived. (p. 38)

This is in striking contrast to the opinions discussed earlier in this chapter . Here the folk constitute not a national group bound together by a common culture, but an ill-defined population of idyllic innocents whose sole characteristic is simplicity. Rousseau is responsible for this model. But both this mythical peasant and the ensuing notion of a fairy tale untouched by its social or historical context are ridiculous. Yet these are the very premises upon which very influential and popular theories of the fairy tale have been built. Their unfortunate success lies in their reassuring appeal to our humanity, to the soothing promise that both human beings and values transcend time and space. In other words, as vessels of purportedly universal human truths, fairy tales belong to us all. The classic example of this view is Bruno Bettelheim, whose popular psychoanalytic interpretations of fairy tales by the Brothers Grimm and Perrault have been widely and enthusiastically embraced.

BETTELHEIM'S PSYCHOANALYTIC INTERPRETATIONS OF FAIRY TALES

From Bettelheim's psychoanalytic perspective, fairy tales address "essential human problems" and "have great psychological meaning" (Bettelheim, 1976, p. 17). Through fairy tales, Bettelheim argues, both children and adults can find their way through life's existential dilemmas. Bettelheim can come to these conclusions because he assumes that fairy tales transcend the specific time and place of their origin and give us insight into "manifold truths . . . which can guide our lives; . . . truth as valid today as it was once upon a time" (p. 310). Thus, fairy tales, whether German or French, for example, would seem to belong to us all, not simply by virtue of our sharing a common Western culture, but because the fairy tale's transcendent nature addresses our common humanity. However, Bettelheim's point of view is problematic because what he believes to be universal truths ultimately turn out to be the values of 19th-century Europe.

The repressive moralizing inherent in Bettelheim's readings of fairy tales has been solidly criticized before, but I mention the issue again here because his understanding of fairy tales remains influential, especially among teachers and children's librarians who often rely on his work. (See Bettelheim, 1987; Flatter, 1985.) Jack Zipes's (1979/1984) criticism of Bettelheim's "Use and Abuse of Folk and Fairy Tales with Children," in particular, deserves reading or rereading in light of the recent, sobering allegations by one of Bettelheim's former patients at the Orthogenic School that the author of *The Uses of Enchantment* was an authoritarian who physically and emotionally abused children in his care (Pekow, 1990; see also Zipes, 1988, pp. 110–134). The values that Bettelheim views as timeless and common to us all frequently turn out to be those of the authoritarian, patriarchal society in which he was raised (Haase, 1991).

Some of Bettelheim's influence has been mitigated by recent studies that reveal the specific sociocultural roots of many tales and thus expose their historically determined values. In fact, for the last 15 years the Grimms' tales have been the center of considerable discussion and controversy as a result of renewed interest in evidence that the Grimms did not give us authentic, unaltered folktales transcribed from the mouths of simple people, but instead drew many of their tales from highly educated informants or printed literary texts. (See Bottigheimer 1987, 1989; Rölleke, 1985; Tater, 1987; Zipes, 1988.) That Wilhelm Grimm had freely revised, edited, added to, and basically rewritten many of the classic tales to reflect his own aesthetic and moral values renders the universal, transcendent view of these tales untenable.

But the discrediting of theories has affected not only those who, like Bettelheim, believe in the universal nature of fairy tales. The nationalists have had to confront the discovery that many of the best known and most cherished of the Grimms' tales are not purely German. They are in many cases of mixed origin. Some of the Grimms' most significant informants have turned out to be educated bourgeois women from families of French Huguenots who had settled in Germany after the revocation of the Edict of Nantes. Of course, to say that these oral sources spoke French and were familiar with the tales of Perrault is not to say that what the Grimms have given us is a collection of French tales. They did not. But it is enough to undermine the view that makes fairy tales the possession of a single nationality.

We are left, however, with a question. If fairy tales are not the universal possession of an all-encompassing, undifferentiated humanity, and if they are not the sole property of any single national group, then to whom do fairy tales belong? This question can be best answered by turning first to the question: Why does it matter at all to whom fairy tales belong?

THE QUESTION OF OWNERSHIP

The question of ownership is not an idle question. As we've seen, our specific views on the origin and nature of fairy tales necessarily imply that we have, implicitly or explicitly, a specific attitude toward their ownership. And these attitudes, in turn, have an impact on the reception of fairy tales insofar as they determine how we both read and use fairy tales. The problem—indeed, the danger—with both the nationalistic/ethnic and universal views of fairy tales is that they prescribe forms of thought and behavior, and modes and models of humanity, that are meant to be normative. That is, they stereotype us—either as members of a nationalistic or ethnic group, or as human beings defined by a certain concept of what is or is not normal. This is why fairy tales have been so frequently utilized by *both* nationalists and universalists in the socialization of children. In both cases, fairy tales are supposed to depict or prescribe for us what is true, as well as what forms of behavior are typical, normal, and acceptable. Whether we view them as yours and mine or as ours, fairy tales—read from these perspectives—confine and limit us, narrowing our views of reality while allegedly giving us greater insight into the other, into ourselves, or into humanity. From these perspectives, fairy tales own us, we don't own them.

An important twist was added to the question of ownership with the proliferation of both printed texts and copyright law in the 19th century. While folktales remain in the public domain because of their anonymous origin in the oral tradition (which accounts in part for their popularity among publishers), there has been a growing tendency to stress private ownership by individuals or even corporations. This is evident in the way we speak about fairy tales. With deference to the folk's public ownership of fairy tales, the Grimms claimed only to have *collected* the stories in their famous edition. Yet we refer to them as "Grimms' fairy tales." Contemporary storytellers, who work for a fee and are cautious about allowing audio or video recordings of their performances, frequently talk of making a traditional folktale their own. Although this is in one sense an artistic claim, the vocabulary of ownership clearly implies the expectation to control and profit from the tale in question. When Disney called his animated fairy tales by his own name—*Walt Disney's Snow White and the Seven Dwarfs, Walt Disney's Sleeping Beauty,* and so on—he was not simply making an artistic statement, but also laying claim to the tales in what would become their most widely known, public versions. In 1989, when the Academy of Motion Picture Arts and Sciences used the figure of Snow White in its televised award ceremonies, the Walt Disney Company filed a lawsuit claiming "unauthorized use of its Snow White character," which the corporation felt had been treated in an unflattering manner in the comical and mildly satirical sketch ("Disney Company," 1989; see also Harmetz, 1989). When the Walt Disney Company spent $1 million for the videocassette rights to the "Rocky and Bullwinkle" series—including the "Fractured Fairy Tales" that sometimes parody the Disney versions and Walt Disney himself—its corporate ownership and control of the fairy tale were extended to even the subversive fairy tale (Kaplan, 1989). If the Walt Disney Company cannot completely prevent unflattering parodies of its fairy-tale movies and their creator, at least it will now be able to control and profit from their distribution.

The Disney case demonstrates that the question of ownership is important because it is ultimately a question of control. So who owns fairy tales? To be blunt: I do. And you do. We can each claim fairy tales for ourselves. Not as members of a national or ethnic folk group—as French, German, or

American. Not as nameless faces in a sea of humanity. And not in the Disney model as legal copyright holders. We claim fairy tales in every individual act of telling and reading. If we avoid reading fairy tales as models of behavior and normalcy, they can become for us revolutionary documents that encourage the development of personal autonomy.

As some revisionist writers and storytellers have already recognized, the removal of the fairy tale from the service of nationalism and universalism requires the subversion of traditional tales. Thus we find contemporary literary versions of "Little Red Riding Hood," for instance, that offer alternative visions. In one version, by the Merseyside Fairy Story Collective, a young girl overcomes her fear and slays the wolf who threatens her grandmother (Zipes, 1983b, pp. 239–246). In another, by Angela Carter, a young woman, far from becoming the wolf's innocent victim, accepts her animal nature—her sexuality—and actually leaves her family and village to join the company of wolves (Zipes, 1983b, pp. 272–280). In other media, such as film, video, and music, attempts have also been made to reclaim the fairy tale. In fact, Angela Carter's Red Riding Hood story, "The Company of Wolves," has itself been remade as a movie (Carter & Jordan, 1984/1985). And some of the irreverent video adaptations in Shelley Duvall's *Fairie Tale Theatre* (1982–85) go a long way toward offsetting the saccharine Disney model of the Consumer Romance. Even in popular music the Disney claim on meaning has been challenged by authorized remakes of the songs from Walt Disney's fairy-tale movies. Sinéad O'Connor's subtly ironic rendering of "Someday My Prince Will Come," Betty Carter's sensual subversion of "I'm Wishing," and Tom Waits's industrialized "Heigh Ho" give us the opportunity to reinterpret Disney and "his" tales for ourselves and our time (Willner, 1988).

DISCOVERING INDIVIDUAL OWNERSHIP OF FAIRY TALES

The opportunity to reclaim fairy tales is as crucial for children as it is for adults. But the right to ownership of the tales may in some ways be more difficult for children to claim. After all, teachers, librarians, parents, and powers in the culture industry exert a certain control over the popular reception of fairy tales by determining to a great extent not only the nature of the tales that are made accessible to children, but also the context of their reception. A storyteller who buys into myths about the pristine origin of fairy tales assumes an unearned mantle of authority and shrouds the stories not only in mystery but in error. A parent under Bruno Bettelheim's spell uses time-bound tales to justify a timeless moral authority. And a teacher concerned about the so-called crisis of cultural literacy will emphasize canonized fairy-tale texts and treat them as sacred cultural artifacts. In each case, children's responses are expected to conform to the external authority of the tales they read or hear. It is no accident that parents and educators so often praise fairy tales because of their ability to enchant children. Stripped of sentimentality, enchantment—that is, being spellbound and powerless—is also a curse. We applaud the rescue of a Frog King or a Sleeping Beauty who is powerless to break the spell of a malevolent force, but when a moralistic text "enchants" and has a child in its spell, we apparently have that child exactly where we want her or him.

There are at least two ways in which children can be awakened from this form of enchantment and helped to discover their individual ownership of fairy tales. First, teachers and parents can offer children a wider variety of fairy tales than is usually proffered. Complementing the classic tales and anthologies with newer or lesser-known stories and variants places the traditional tales in a context that encourages diverse responses, questions, and significant comparisons—even among elementary school children. When I read my own daughter the Grimms' "Little Red Riding Hood" and the version of the Merseyside Fairy Story Collective, for example, she announced that she liked the second version better "because the little girl was smarter."

Numerous anthologies that resurrect neglected fairy tales and offer alternatives to the best-known classic tales are readily available today. Among them are Alison Lurie's (1980) *Clever Gretchen and Other Forgotten Folktales*, Ethel Johnston Phelps's (1981) *The Maid of the North: Feminist Folktales from Around the World,* and Suzanne I. Barchers's (1990) *Wise Women: Folk and Fairy Tales from Around the World.* Each of these seeks to provide tales with female characters who resist the stereotypes that dominate the fairy-tale market. Jack Zipes (1983b, 1986) has the same goal in *The Trials and Tribulations of Little Red Riding Hood: Versions of the Tale in Sociocultural Context* and *Don't Bet on the Prince: Contemporary Feminist Fairy Tales in North America and England.* Both of these also include significant bibliographies of many other alternative fairy tales. The traditional fairy-tale canon can also be complemented by stories "belonging" to other cultural traditions. Virginia Hamilton's (1985) *The People Could Fly,* for example, is an excellent anthology of American Black folktales that can be reclaimed by new generations. Innovative illustrations can also recast a familiar text in such a way as to allow children fresh responses to a classic story. In Creative Education's fairy-tale series, for example, Sarah Moon (1983) has outfitted Perrault's *Little Red Riding Hood* with haunting—for some perhaps troubling—black and white photographs that reinterpret the story for the urban reader. Of video and film versions of fairy tales, teachers might want to explore Tom Davenport's innovative but uneven series *From the Brothers Grimm: American Versions of Folktale Classics* (1975–89), which now consists of nine Grimm tales transplanted into American settings. Whereas Davenport's film adaptations combine reverence for the tales with moments of humor, Roald Dahl's (1983/1986) *Revolting Rhymes* openly demystifies classic tales. Dahl's irreverent fairy-tale adaptations in verse are a good antidote to the saccharine presentations often found in children's editions. In fact, Dahl has a firm sense of what "enchantment" is and how to break it, as witnessed in these opening lines from "Cinderella":

> I guess you think you know this story.
> You don't. The real one's much more gory.
> The phoney one, the one you know,
> Was cooked up years and years ago,
> And made to sound all soft and sappy
> Just to keep the children happy. (p. 1)

Beyond presenting children with a variety of fairy tales, adults can also encourage the creative reception of fairy tales. In other words, children can make fairy tales their own by creating and re-creating their own versions. There is good evidence that given the opportunity, children will take fairy tales into their own hands in any case. In his book on the Brothers Grimm, Jack Zipes (1988) has recounted how fifth- and sixth-grade girls combined the character of Peter Pumpkin-Eater and the story of Cinderella into a new tale that explicitly reflects their developing sexuality and consciousness (p. 146). And Kristin Wardetzky (1990) has shown how the storytelling of children in the former East Germany does not always succumb to the dominant cultural models and re-creates the fairy tale in ways that express the children's power over the genre.

At the end of his list of heresies Wolfdietrich Schnurre (1978/1986) wonders, "Can the fairy tale be saved?" His answer: "Perhaps. If specialists expose the roots of the tales and tell them in a way that is thoroughly new and which expresses their essence" (p. 25). Writers and professional storytellers retelling tales and making them their own can indeed renew the fairy tale. But readers, too—including children—can reread and reinterpret the tales in new ways. By experiencing a wide variety of tales, they can view the stories of the classical canon in new contexts. By actively selecting, discussing, enacting, illustrating, adapting, and retelling the tales they experience, both adults and children can assert their own proprietary rights to meaning. It is no heresy to re-appropriate the tales from either tradition or the culture industry. "They are not," as Auden (1944) knew, "sacred texts" (p. 28). If the fairy tale needs saving and if we are to save it, then we need to abandon the untenable views of its ownership that put us in its power.

We must take possession of it on our own terms. Saving the fairy tale in this way is nothing less than saving our very selves.

REFERENCES

Auden, W. H. (1944, November 12). In Praise of the Brothers Grimm [Review of *Grimm's Fairy Tales*]. *The New York Times Book Review*, pp. 1, 28.

Barchers, S. I. (1990). *Wise women: Folk and fairy tales from around the world.* Englewood, CO: Libraries Unlimited.

Bausinger, H. (1980). Anmerkungen zu Schneewittchen. In H. Brackert (Ed.), *Und wenn sie nicht gestorben sind: Perspektiven auf das Märchen* (pp. 39–70). Frankfurt: Suhrkamp.

Becker, J. (1985). Der hilflose Anti-Faschismus. *Hessische Blätter für Volks- und Kulturforschung*, n.s. *18*, 117–119.

Bettelheim, B. (1976). *The uses of enchantment: The meaning and importance of fairy tales.* New York: Knopf.

Bettelheim, B. (1987, January). Children and fairy tales. *Pre-K*, p. 21.

Bottigheimer, R. B. (1987). *Grimms' bad girls and bold boys: The moral and social vision of the tales.* New Haven, CT: Yale University Press.

Bottigheimer, R. B. (1989). Fairy tales, folk narrative research and history. *Social History, 14*, 343–357.

Brun, V. (1939). The German fairy tale. *Menorah Journal, 27*, 147–155.

Carter, A., & Jordan, N. (Screenwriters). (1985). *The company of wolves* [Videotape]. Vestron Video. (Original work produced 1984)

Cocchiara, G. (1981). *The history of folklore in Europe.* Translated by J. N. McDaniel. Philadelphia: Institute for the Study of Human Issues. (Original work published 1952)

Dahl, R. (1986). *Revolting rhymes.* Toronto: Bantam. (Original work published 1983)

Darnton, R. (1984). Peasants tell tales: The meaning of Mother Goose. In R. Darnton, *The great cat massacre and other episodes in French cultural history* (pp. 9–72, 265–270). New York: Basic Books.

Davenport, T. (Producer and director). (1975–89). *From the Brothers Grimm: American Versions of Folktale Classics.* [Videotape series]. Davenport Films.

Disney Company sues over Snow White use. (1989, March 31). *New York Times,* p. C33.

Dundes, A. (1965). *The study of folklore.* Englewood Cliffs, NJ: Prentice Hall.

Duvall, S. (Producer). (1982–85). *Fairie Tale Theatre.* [Videotape series]. Playhouse Video.

Flatter, C. H. (1985, Summer). Folktales: The enchanted lesson. *American Educator*, pp. 30–33.

Haase, D. (1988). Gold into straw: Fairy tale movies for children and the culture industry. *The Lion and the Unicorn, 12*(2), 193–207.

Haase, D. (1991). "Verzauberungen der Seele": Das Märchen und die Exilanten der NS-Zeit. In E. Iwasaki (Ed.), *Begegnung mit dem "Fremden": Grenzen—Trad-*

itionen—Vergleiche: Akten des VIII. Internationalen Germanisten-Kongresses, Tokyo 1990 (Vol. 8, pp. 44–50). Munich: iudicium.

Hamilton, V. (1985). *The people could fly.* New York: Knopf.

Harmetz, A. (1989, April 7). An apology to Disney. *New York Times,* p. C30.

Hazard, P. (1947). *Books, children and men.* Translated by Marguerite Mitchell. Boston: Horn Book.

Heyer, S. (1985). *Hessische Blätter für Volks- und Kulturforschung,* n.s. *18,* 111–116. (Original work by T. J. Leonard published 1947)

Kamenetsky, C. (1972). Folklore as a political tool in Nazi Germany. *Journal of American Folklore, 85,* 221–235.

Kamenetsky, C. (1977). Folktale and ideology in the Third Reich. *Journal of American Folklore, 90,* 168–178.

Kamenetsky, C. (1984). *Children's literature in Hitler's Germany.* Athens: Ohio University Press.

Kaplan, D. A. (1989, May 7). Vatch out Natasha, Moose and Squirrel are back. *Detroit Free Press,* p. 3F.

Leonard, T. J. (1947). First steps in cruelty. *British Zone Review: A Fortnightly Review of the Activities of the Control Commission for Germany (B.E.) and Military Government, 1*(37), 10–13.

Lurie, A. (1980). *Clever Gretchen and other forgotten folktales.* New York: Crowell.

Mallet, C.-H. (1984). *Fairy tales and children: The psychology of children revealed through four of Grimm's fairy tales.* Translated by J. Neugroschel. New York: Schocken.

Moon, S. (Illustrator). (1983). *Little Red Riding Hood.* Mankato, MN: Creative Education.

Pekow, C. (1990, August 26). The other Dr. Bettelheim: The revered psychologist had a dark, violent side. *Washington Post,* pp. C1, C4.

Phelps, E. J. (1981). *The maid of the north: Feminist folktales from around the world.* New York: Holt, Rinehart and Winston.

Rölleke, Heinz. (1985). *Die Märchen der Brüder Grimm: Eine Einführung.* Munich: Artemis.

Sainte-Beuve, C.-A. (1944). Charles Perrault. In C.-A. Sainte-Beuve, *Causeries du lundi* (Vol. 5, pp. 255–274). Paris: Garnier. (Original work published in 1851)

Schnurre, W. (1986). Ketzerisches zum Märchenschatz: 24 kurzweilige Thesen. In W. Mieder (Ed.), *Grimmige Märchen: Prosatexte von Ilse Aichinger bis Martin Walser* (pp. 21–25). Frankfurt: Fischer. (Original work published 1978)

Snyder, L. L. (1978). Cultural nationalism: The Grimm Brothers' fairy tales. In L. L. Snyder, *Roots of German nationalism* (pp. 35–54). Bloomington: Indiana University Press. (Reprint of Nationalistic aspects of the Grimm Brothers' fairy tales, *Journal of Social Psychology,* 1951, *33,* 209–223)

Tatar, M. (1987). *The hard facts of the Grimms' fairy tales.* Princeton: Princeton University Press.

Wardetzky, K. (1990). The structure and interpretation of fairy tales composed by children. *Journal of American Folklore, 103,* 157–176.

Willner, H. (Producer). (1988). *Stay awake: Various interpretations of music from vintage Disney films* [Audiotape]. A & M.

Zipes, J. (1983a). *Fairy tales and the art of subversion: The classical genre for children and the process of civilization.* New York: Wildman.

Zipes, J. (Ed.). (1983b). *The trials and tribulations of Little Red Riding Hood: Versions of the tale in sociocultural context.* South Hadley, MA: Bergin & Garvey.

Zipes, J. (1984). On the use and abuse of folk and fairy tales with children: Bruno Bettelheim's moralistic magic wand. In J. Zipes, *Breaking the magic spell: Radical theories of folk and fairy tales* (pp. 160–182). New York: Methuen. (Original work published 1979)

Zipes, J. (Ed.). (1986). *Don't bet on the prince: Contemporary feminist fairy tales in North America and England.* New York: Methuen.

Zipes, J. (1988). *The Brothers Grimm: From enchanted forests to the modern world.* New York: Routledge.

TRY THIS

Read a fairy tale to your class, for instance, "Snow White and the Seven Dwarfs." Then show the group an updated version of the same story, for instance, *Snow White in New York.* (See below for additional updated stories.) Encourage your class to write their own "fractured folktales."

—G.B.

BIBLIOGRAPHY

These Selected Stories are Spinoffs of Traditional Folktales

Aylesworth, J. (1990). *The completed hickory dickory dock.* Illustrated by Eileen Christelow. New York: Atheneum.

Emberley, M. (1990). *Ruby.* Boston: Little, Brown.

French, F. (1986). *Snow White in New York.* New York: Oxford University Press.

Grimm, J., & Grimm, W. K. (1981). *Hansel and Gretel.* Illustrated by Anthony Browne. New York: Knopf.

Gwynne, F. *Pondlarker.* (1990). New York: Simon & Schuster.

Hennessy, B. G. (1990). *Eeney, meeney, miney, mo.* Illustrated by Letizia Galli. New York: Viking Penguin.

Ivemey, J. W. (1990). *The complete story of the three blind mice.* Illustrated by Victoria Chess. Boston: Little, Brown.

Kimmel, E. (1991). *Bearhead.* Illustrated by Charles Mikolaycak. New York: Holiday House.

Kellogg, S. (1985). *Chicken Little.* New York: Mulberry.

Kovalski, M. (1991). *Pizza for breakfast.* New York: Morrow.

Lobel, A. (1980). *Fables.* New York: Harper & Row.

Marshall, J. (1991). *Old Mother Hubbard and her wonderful dog.* Illustrated by James Marshall. New York: Farrar, Straus & Giroux.

Scieszka, J. (1989). *The true story of the three little pigs by A. Wolf.* New York: Viking Penguin.

Scieszka, J. (1991). *The frog prince continued.* Illustrated by Steve Johnson. New York: Viking Penguin.

Turkle, B. (1976). *Deep in the forest.* New York: Dutton.

Ungerer, T. (1974). *Allumette.* New York: Methuen.

Williams, J. (1973). *Petronella.* Illustrated by Friso Henstra. New York: Parents Magazine Press.

Williams, J. (1979). *The practical princess and other liberating tales.* Illustrated by Rick Schreiter New York: Parents Magazine Press.

Yeoman, John. (1990). *Old Mother Hubbard's dog learns to play.* Illustrated by Quentin Blake. Boston: Houghton Mifflin.

Yolen, J. (1981a). *The acorn quest.* Illustrated by Susanna Nati. New York: Crowell.

Yolen, J. (1981b). *Sleeping ugly.* Illustrated by Diane Stanley. New York: Knopf.

Yolen, J. (1990). *Baby Bear's bedtime book.* Illustrated by Jane Dyer. New York: Harcourt Brace Jovanovich.

Yorinks, A. (1990). *Ugh.* Illustrated by Richard Egielski. New York: Farrar, Straus & Giroux.

Zipes, J. (1986). *Don't bet on the prince: Contemporary feminist fairy tales in North America and England.* New York: Methuen.

CHAPTER 6

❖ FOLKTALE VARIANTS: LINKS TO THE NEVER-ENDING CHAIN

Patricia J. Cianciolo

Folktales often bear a striking family resemblance to each other, somehow alike and yet not quite identical. A typical example is "The Gingerbread Boy," a story with a number of fairytale "relatives," which are similar and yet not quite the same. "The Journey Cake, Ho," is an American tale about the travels of a "journey cake," a common food in Colonial America; a second story, "The Bun," from Russia, is about a runaway bun; a third, "The Bannock," is a Scottish story about the travels of an oatmeal cake. Although the tales are similar in a number of ways, the runaway food is always that which is commonly eaten by the people who told the story.

The four tales are also alike in another way. Whenever the food encounters someone new, it announces that it has run away and escaped a number of individuals, and that it cannot be caught. With each retelling the runaway recites a cumulative poem similar to the one below:

I've run away from a little old woman,
A little old man,
A barn full of threshers,
And I can run away from you, I can!

Although the foods say much the same thing, the endings are different in at least one respect. As the cakes and breads are being eaten, all except the pancake recite a rhyme similar to the following:

Oh dear! I'm quarter gone!
Oh! I'm half gone!
Oh! I'm three quarters done.
Oh! I'm all gone!

suggesting that the fox or the wolf is taking a series of bites out of it. Only the pancake has nothing to say at all because the wily fox swallows it in a single gulp.

Scholars have long been interested in similarities and differences among folktales: folklorists as keys to individual cultures, historians as reflections of the human experience, literary scholars as guides to understanding literature. Teachers, however, in their work with children, have not always taken full advantage of the similarities and differences among folktales. Some point out parallel fairy tales; but few emphasize important ties between cultures and stories, and as a result they fail to take full advantage of the tales.

In this interesting chapter, Dr. Patricia J. Cianciolo describes some fresh approaches teachers can use to help children explore fairy tales and their connection with the culture reflected in the tales. The effects are satisfying for everyone concerned.

It is common these days to see folktales being read in elementary school classrooms. Sometimes they are used to entertain, at other times to teach reading skills, and at still others to help children understand the characteristics of literary genre. Folktales are even used to promote standards of behavior or cultural pluralism.

One teacher working in a school attended by children from various regions in the United States and foreign countries began the school year with an oral reading of folktales from each country or region represented in the class. She also took photographs of each child and placed the pictures on a globe in the appropriate country or region. She then attached a brightly colored ribbon to the location and connected it to a picture-book retelling of the folktale from the same country or region. Within a few short weeks, she had honored every child with a reading of a folktale from his or her homeland or region.

In another classroom, a teacher first read a number of "Rumpelstiltskin" variants from different locations and then helped students record the likenesses and differences among the stories on a Comparison Chart similar to the one in the "Try This" section at the end of this chapter (p. 000). All of the variants contained a supernatural helper whose name was guessed by the protagonist: King Olav, Master Builder of Seljord Church (Christiansen, 1964), a Norwegian tale (a troll called Skaane magically assists the girl in this story); "The Lazy Spinning Girl Who Became Queen" (Degh, 1969), a Magyar tale (the magic helper in the tale is a little man named Dancing Vargaluska); and "The Pretty but Idle Girl" (Yearsley, 1968), a Basque story (a witch called Marie Kirikitoun uses magic to help the girl in this tale). On their own the children also read *Tom Tit Tot,* an English tale from the East Anglia area retold and illustrated by Eveline Ness (1965); *Duffy and the Devil,* a Cornish tale retold by Harve Zemach and illustrated by Margot Zemach (1973); and *Rumpelstiltskin,* the Grimm brothers' story retold and illustrated by Donna Diamond (1983).

The Comparison Chart helped the children understand the similarities and differences among the stories by highlighting story elements, or *motifs,* that were repeated in story after story. The teacher also pointed out that some of the stories had motifs that were different from the others, making the chart useful as a springboard for discussion and as a guide for reading, comparing, and categorizing the tales by motif and country.

By connecting the children, their ethnic or cultural heritage, and the geographic location of the stories, the teacher helped unify the group while focusing on individual children within it. The emphasis on cultural heritage and geography encouraged the youngsters to take pride in their respective heritages. It also helped them grasp the idea that people have always told stories about their experiences, feelings, and relationships with one another, and that the stories are shaped by the human experience, which is always assimilated in every retelling. In other words, the children learned that the tales are shaped by the place in which the storytellers live, by the customs and moral outlook of the people who tell the stories, as well as by the values of the group. The heroes, ideals, wishes, and even the images people create are affected by the place and culture from which the storytellers sprang.

THE FOLKLORE PROCESS

The work with the children, the connections between the fairy-tale variants, and the recognition of different cultures were also important because the three are links to a never-ending chain of folklore. From the beginnings of mankind, stories were always told and then passed from narrator to narrator, each storyteller adding his personal touch by changing the story to suit himself. The stories were recast whenever the storyteller wanted the story to fit the setting and values at home. Expressions and images were touched up or altered; incompatible or conflicting voices were given stylistic unity. The results were variants of the first story. As people traveled from place to place by caravan or ship, in explorations and in wars, they told their own stories and heard others.

The same phenomenon occurs today. As people move from one community to another across countries and seas from one coast to another, their stories are transplanted and cross-fertilized as they are shared informally with new acquaintances. All sorts of people help them: professional storytellers, book publishers, producers of commercial films and television programs. As a result, ethnic and cultural traditions are reflected in the stories.

Humanity's dreams and aspirations, strengths and frailties, thoughts and feelings are always embedded in these narratives because, like all narrative literature, they are fictionalized reflections of real life. But as fiction they are more than mere reflections of life because the storyteller shapes the tale in some way: as a fairy tale, a legend, as historical or modern realistic fiction. The story is therefore an illusion of reality, not a real human experience or even a replication or facsimile. A well-crafted tale effectively shared thus has the potential to provide listeners or readers with an aesthetic experience.

An important aesthetic feature of folktales is that the stories are often similar. Many begin and end the same way; heroes often win in spite of a variety of disadvantages; many heroines suffer passively and win in the end. The similarities play an important role in the way storytellers tell tales. Listeners know what to expect at the beginning and the end of the story; they recognize repeated rhymes and descriptions. Indeed, the repeated phrases and clauses become cues for the storytellers.

The events of the story also seem similar to real life. Because the description is minimal, because the terminology is general and the setting timeless and remote, anything seems possible in the imprecise realms of far away. Listeners go away from the story with the feeling that what happens could happen again in today's world but to someone else. So events, however fearful, are distanced from the listener or reader, partly because the similarities play an important role for the storytellers and listeners.

Outstanding features of the culture from which the story sprang become apparent because they are so often similar. When the same elements are repeated in one tale after another, small differences between them become all the more prominent, all the more obvious as features of a specific culture. Because the stories are compatible with the morals, beliefs, ideals, traditions, even the humor of a people who told the story, they seem perfectly suited to their culture of origin. The similarities thus play an important role for the storytellers and listeners alike.

Underlying morals also play a role in the ease with which the story is accepted. When the simple virtues of the good characters are victorious and the equally simple and perverse wrongdoers are punished, when the outcome is uncomplicated and predictable, the story is basically very satisfying and comforting. Although morals are rarely presented in a didactic manner (except in fables), good and evil are clearly delineated although not by means of sophisticated symbolism. The wellsprings of basic feelings, drives, and needs embedded in the folktale's motifs and archetypes give listeners a comprehensive view of life.

Proof of the connection between stories and people can be found in ourselves. Psychologists insist that the patterns of behavior described in folktales are present in our imagination, even in our dreams. Indeed, psychologist Sam Keen, writing in *Psychology Today* (1988), reports that people often invent characters who resemble well-known folklore figures in their dreams.

Proof of the basic connection between folklore and people also lies in the names of characters. Often they are simply known generically as "the king," "the queen," "the youngest daughter," or "the oldest son," although specific names may be reserved for the hero and/or heroine and perhaps the antagonist. Even then, the names tend to point to the characters as types of Everyman: "Goldilocks," "Snow White," "Cinderella," and "Tattercoats."

Proof of the connection between people and the folklore process is also found in the language itself because it generally reflects the locale from which the story comes. Because folk stories are traditionally told by members of the local community—by the mother or father in one's home, by an elder at an extended family gathering, or by a storyteller sharing tales with others in a local meeting place, the language usually reflects the speech of the locale, as well the idiom of an individual teller. The story may contain catch phrases and set descriptions derived from oral tradition, and even when the retelling is a written recording of an oral tale or a translation, the spontaneity, rhythm and syntax, the distinctive and subtle colloquialisms used by the teller can be retained if the work of transcription is carefully done.

Because the stories originated and were transmitted from one person to another, from one culture to another, it is clear why there often are variants of traditional fairy tales and why the differences are important. Even when there is a certain sameness about variants of tales as "Cinderella," "Rumpelstiltskin," "Tom Thumb" and "The Crane Wife," in the variations lie keys to the ethnic or culture groups that originally told the stories.

THE CINDERELLA STORIES

We can understand the process more clearly by a close look at some folktales, for example, the "Cinderella" stories, one of the most widespread and popular fairy tales throughout the world. Numerous versions of "Cinderella" have been located. Miriam Coxan analyzed 345 versions of this tale (Coxan, 1893); Anna Rooth studied 900 versions from Europe and Asia (Rooth, 1951).

Although the stories come from all over the world, all are similar in certain ways. Each one is about an abused, neglected, or rejected girl: in each, the heroine is expected to do hard work and/or to complete a seemingly impossible task. In some, a magic, benevolent person, creature, or object helps the Cinderella character realize her dreams. In fact, in most variants the benefactor seems to control the life and destiny of the girl and affects the fate of all the mortals in the story, as well as acting benevolently (or malevolently if he/she/it has been displeased.)

In the well-known French version retold by Perrault (1697), Cendrillon (Cinderella) works constantly for her stepmother and stepsisters even though she is a daughter of the house. She sleeps in a garret on a straw pallet, sits among cinders to keep warm and dreams of a better life. We all know that with the help of a fairy godmother, her dreams ultimately come true.

Russian and Chinese Variants

Vassilisa and Yeh-Shen, the respective Russian and southern Chinese Cinderella heroines, find themselves in situations comparable to Cendrillon's. Recent picture-book retellings of these folktales are *Lovely Vassilisa,* retold by Barbara Cohen and illustrated by Anatoly Ivanhoff (1990), and *Yeh-Shen,* retold by Ai-Ling Louie and illustrated by Ed Young (1982). Forced to work hard by her stepmother and two step-sisters, Vassilisa is able to win her prince with the help of the doll who is her constant companion and helper. At the beginning of the story, Vassilisa's task is to go to the fearsome Baba Yaga to get a flame with which to light candles. Baba Yaga first tells the girl to complete some tasks: weed the vegetable garden, light the fires for heating water and cooking food, pick out black bits from the millet, remove the dirt from the poppy seeds, and cook the meals. Because Vassilisa completes each task perfectly with the help of the doll, the old witch sends her home with a skull whose glowing eyes provide the light her stepmother and stepsisters wanted. The skull then burns them to a cinder in retribution for their cruelty to Vassilisa.

Afterwards, Vassilisa goes to live with an old woman and there weaves a most beautiful cloth, which the old woman then gives to the Tsar. He asks the weaver to make it into shirts for him. When he summons the girl to reward her, he falls in love with her and marries her.

Although Yeh-Shen, the heroine of a T'ang dynasty (A.D. 618–907) variant, is the orphaned daughter of a cave chief, her stepmother forces her to do the heaviest and most unpleasant chores (Louie, 1982). With the help of the magic bones from a pet fish her stepmother has killed, Yeh-Shen attends the spring festival dressed in a gown of azure blue, a cloak of kingfisher feathers draped around her shoulders. On her feet are slippers woven of golden threads in a pattern like the scales of her beloved pet fish, and soles made of solid gold.

When, like Cendrillon, Yeh-Shen loses her slipper as she runs away from the festivities, the king tries to find the owner by displaying the slipper on the pavilion where it was found so that its owner can claim it. In the darkest part of the night Yeh-Shen comes to the pavilion to snatch the shoe, for she wants to return it, along with its mate, to the fish. The king orders his men to follow the girl when he notices her tiny feet and is impressed with the difference between her fine features and her tattered clothes. When the king later tells her to try on the golden slippers and she puts them on, her clothes are immediately transformed into the elegant outfit she had worn to the festival.

Yeh-Shen and the king are happily married, but the king is not so kind to Yeh-Shen's family. He does not allow them to move to the palace, and shortly afterwards her stepmother and her stepsister are crushed to death when their cave collapses.

Not all of the Cinderella variants adhere so closely to the pattern of the tales described above, yet their images and themes express the same underlying meaning. In variants from Canada, Czechoslovakia, Africa, and Japan, the heroines accomplish impossible tasks.

Native American Variant

"Burnt Face," the Native American variant of Cinderella from Canada retold by DeWit (1979) in *The Talking Stone: An Anthology of Native American Tales and Legends,* combines the rags-to-riches theme with a *"pourquoi"* story that tells why the leaves of the aspen trees tremble even in the most gentle wind. In this tale, the abused heroine is the youngest daughter of a great chief orphaned when she is very young. Except for her two older sisters, who are jealous of her, the girl is loved by all because of her beauty and because she is gentle and patient, honest and hard-working. Her sisters clothe her in rags to make her ugly, cut off her long black hair, and burn her face with hot coals so that she is scarred and disfigured. They tell their father that she has done it to herself, thus the name "Burnt Face."

In their village there lives a great warrior whose name is Strong Wind the Invisible, who can be seen only by his sister. Burnt Face, like her sisters and all the other maidens in their village, knows that Strong Wind will marry the first maiden who can see him as he comes home to his tent near the sea at night. The test is to see him. Only a truthful maiden can see him and therefore win him.

As he comes home from work each evening at twilight, Strong Wind's sister asks the girl who seeks him if she can see him. When the girl answers falsely, the sister asks the girl to tell her with what he drew his sled. Each time, it is obvious that the girl is only guessing. Having tried and lied and failed, none of the maidens passes the warrior's test.

Everyone laughs at Burnt Face when she resolves to win Strong Wind, but she is the only one who responds truthfully to the questions his sister asks of her, because the warrior is actually visible to her. Not only is she truthful, she is also able to tell his sister that he draws his sled with the Rainbow and that his bowstring is of the Milky Way.

Later, when Strong Wind's sister takes Burnt Face home and bathes her, all the scars disappear. Her black hair grows long, and the sister dresses the girl in fine clothes and ornaments. The next day, Strong Wind marries Burnt Face, who helps him do great deeds ever after. Strong Wind then punishes the girl's sisters by changing them into aspen trees. From that day to the present, the leaves of the aspen trees always quake in fear as Strong Wind approaches, for the girls are forever mindful of his anger with them for their lies and cruelty to Burnt Face. [Slightly different versions of this tale are included in each of two recently published folktale collections: "Little Burnt Face," in *The Talking Stone, An Anthology of Native American Tales and Legends* (de Wit, 1979) and "The Indian Cinderella," in *World Folktales: A Scribner Resource Collection* (Clarkson, Atelia, & Cross, 1980). A stunning picture-book retelling of this variant of Cinderella is available in *The Rough-Faced Girl,* retold by Rafe Martin and illustrated by David Shannon (1992).]

Czechoslovakian Variant

The Native American story about Burnt Face can be likened to "The Month Brothers" (Marshak, 1983), the Czech variant. In this story the heroine also accomplishes an ostensibly impossible task. The heroine, who is referred to only as "the little girl," lives under much the same conditions as Cendrillion. Her stepmother, who is wicked and greedy, also favors her own daughter over the little girl, whom she treats like a servant. Clearly, her stepmother would like to get rid of the little girl altogether; for during the height of a blizzard in January, she orders the girl to go out into the woods to pick a bouquet of snowdrops, flowers that bloom only in March when the winter freeze is over.

Twelve magical brothers, each the master of the weather during a different month of the year, help the girl accomplish the impossible: they accelerate the weather (they may not skip the actual sequence of the seasons), passing through the weather for the months of January and February to the end of March, when the girl is given one hour to fill her basket and her apron with the snowdrop blossoms. When she returns home, her greedy stepmother sends her stepsister out for the same prize. But the girl gets lost in a snowstorm, and later the mother does the same. The heroine lives alone in their house on the edge of the wood. There she marries her true love and lives happily ever after.

Japanese Variant

The Japanese variant of the Cinderella story, "Benizara and Kakezara," retold by Seki (1963) in *Folktales of Japan,* is similar in a number of ways. Tests and ultimate rewards are given for intellectual honesty and truthfulness. In this story, as in most tales, the girls' names indicate their character: Benizara or "Crimson Dish" is honest, gentle, and talented, the child of the former wife, and Kakezara or "Broken Dish," who is ordinary and decidedly lacking in talent, the daughter of the stepmother.

As in other Cinderella stories, the stepmother treats her stepdaughter badly and her own daughter well. The mother sends both girls out to gather chestnuts and tells them not to come back until each has filled her bag. But Benizara is not able to fill her bag no matter how many chestnuts she picks, for it has a hole in the bottom.

Afraid of the dark and reluctant to go home without completing her task, Benizara asks the old woman living in a nearby house if she might spend the night. The old woman explains that she cannot invite her to stay because her sons are *oni,* malevolent superhuman ogres in human form who would eat her up if they found her there. She tells the girl how to find her way home, fills her basket with chestnuts, and gives her a bag of rice and a magic box which she can call upon for help if necessary. She also tells the girl that if she meets the *oni* on the way, Benizara should chew rice and spread it around in her mouth, lie down and pretend she is dead. When Benizara hears the *oni* on their way home, she does as the old woman had directed. The *oni* think she is already dead and being consumed by worms, so they continue on their way.

At home once more, she wants to attend a play in the village, but her stepmother takes only Kakezara to see it, leaving Benizara to finish her work. With the help of friends who want her to go with them to see the play, she finishes her assigned tasks and tells the box she needs a kimono so she can go to the play dressed appropriately.

During the performance a nobleman notices her giving her sister candy; and so, the next day he visits the family home looking for the beautiful girl he saw at the performance. Although the mother insists that he had seen Kakezara, he demands to see the other girl and is presented with the shabbily dressed Benizara.

To determine which girl he actually did see, he asks each to compose a poem describing a scene that he arranged on a tray: a plate filled with salt, a pine cone sitting on it. Kakezara fails to apply the meter arrangement required for the tanka poetic form (5–7–5–7–7 syllables). Benizara's poem, on the other hand, contains a beautiful metaphor and is structured carefully according to the rules for the meter. The lord immediately puts her in the carriage and takes her to his palace. The stepmother shoves the girl into a huge basket because she wants Kakezara to go to the palace, too. She drags her along so violently that Kakezara falls over the edge of a deep gully and dies.

Regional North American Variants

Two stories from the Americas reflect our geography and ethnic backgrounds: *The Talking Eggs: A Folktale from the American South,* a Creole folktale from Louisiana, retold recently by Robert San Souci (1989), and *Moss Gown,* a North Carolina coast Cinderella story retold by William H. Hooks (1987). In *The Talking Eggs,* a widow and her two daughters live on a farm; the younger girl, who is abused by her mother and sister, helps an old woman and is rewarded with magic eggs that produce gold and jewels. When her sister seeks the same riches, the old woman allows her to take eggs that spew out snakes, toads, and vermin. The setting, the characters, the special kind of magic performed by the woman, the very mood of the story are a rich blend of Southern black lore and European sources. *Moss Gown,* known in Eastern North Carolina (the Tidewater region) as "Like Meat Loves Salt," is a version of the Cinderella story known as "Catskins" or "Cap O' Rushes," an English fairy tale that contains "the loving like salt" incident and the heroine in disguise.

An elderly, ailing father spends his days trying to decide how he will divide his plantation lands. There are three daughters, Retha and Grenadine (the two older girls, who are greedy and deceitful) and Candace (the youngest girl, who is honest and loving.) There also is a Gris-gris Woman—a black witch who lives in a swamp—and the Young Master, the son of the owner of the house where Candace serves as a scullery maid.

As in Shakespeare's *King Lear,* this story begins with the father telling his three daughters that he will divide his lands according to the degree his daughters love him when they answer his question, "How much do you love me?" The two older girls respond with extravagant answers; Candace, on the other hand, responds with the modest and allusive answer, "I love you more than meat loves salt."

The father, angry and hurt with her strange answer, orders the girl out of the house and says he will give all his land to Retha and Grenadine. Candace is rescued by the Gris-gris Woman in the swamp, who gives her a fine gown and tells her that the gown holds magic as long as the Morning Star shines. The woman also tells the girl that if she ever needs her, she should say "Gris-gris, gris-gris, grine" and she will appear "as sudden as a firefly." The girl puts on the beautiful gown, but it turns to rags and moss just as the Morning Star fades.

The mistress of a plantation takes pity on the girl and allows her to help with the kitchen chores. Candace, who now calls herself Moss Gown, performs her arduous tasks without complaining. Because the Gris-gris Woman changes the moss gown into an elegant, delicate gown, Candace can attend the three balls held by the Young Master. She dances with him on each of the three consecutive nights but does not tell him her name or where she came from; she always manages to slip away from the ball just before the Morning Star fades and her gown changes back to rags and moss.

The young man searches the countryside for the girl, returning home sad and discouraged because he has failed to find her. He is so sad that he refuses to eat and becomes ill. Moss Gown then gets permission from the First Cook to take him some food. She puts on her ragged dress and calls upon the Gris-gris Woman to change the dress into a fine gown. He recognizes her as the one he danced with and grew to love, and she tells him her sad story. As they talk through the night, the Morning Star fades and her gown turns into rags and moss, but the young man says that tatters can never hide her beauty. They are married in a grand ceremony.

Among the guests is an old man, feeble and almost blind. He lingers after the feast and the servants take him to the kitchen to warm him by the fire. He tells them that his daughters squandered his wealth and then turned him out to sleep in the woods and beg for food. Moss Gown recognizes him as her father, but she realizes that he does not know her. She asks the First Cook to prepare a meal without salt. When the old man predictably pushes the food away, Moss Gown hands him a saltcellar and says, "I love you more than meat loves salt." Thereupon, the old man recognizes his daughter and tells her that he misjudged her. He is invited to live in Moss Gown's home as long as he likes.

Table 6.1 compares and contrasts the eight variants of Cinderella discussed above.

FAIRY TALES: LINKS TO A NEVER-ENDING CHAIN

Folktales encourage young people to take pride in their origins, to highlight how people live today and how they used to live, and to understand their own heritage, for the stories reflect the values, customs, and lifestyles of the people who told the stories. They clearly are of considerable importance to young people.

When teachers use variants of the same story drawn from a number of countries around the world, they can also point to the similarities and differences among the stories and use the stories as keys to understanding the

Table 6.1 Comparisons of Cinderella variants

Title	Setting	Heroine	Sources of abuse/ neglect/rejection	Task	Magic	Results
"Cindrillon"	France; house	Cindrillon	Stepsisters Stepmother	Cleans Obedience	Fairy Godmother	Stepfamily punished; heroine marries prince
"Yeh-Shen"	Canton (China); Cave	Yeh-Shen	Stepmother Stepsister	Cleans; endures abuse gracefully	Fish bones	Cave collapses marries lord
"Vasillisa"	Russia; house in the woods	Vasillisa	Stepmother Stepsisters	Got flame from Baba Yaga; Skillfullness	Doll	Stepfamily burned; heroine weds tsar
"Burnt Face"	North America; (Canada); tent	Burnt Face	Sisters	See invisible; man; truth-fullness	Warrior is invisible	Sisters changed into Aspen trees; heroine marries warrior
"The Month Brothers"	Czechoslavakian woods	Little girl	Stepsister Stepmother	Bring home snowdrop blossoms in January; Obedience	Accelerate seasons of the year	Twelve Month Brothers control weather and seasonal changes
"Benizara and Kakezara"	Japan; house	Benizara (Crimson Dish)	Stepsister Stepmother	Collect chestnuts and create poems	Magic box	Stepsister falls into gully; Heroine marries nobleman
"The Talking Eggs"	Louisiana (rural) Creole	Blanch	Mothers and sisters	Chores; Kindness	Magic eggs	Mother and sister punished; heroine goes to the city and lives like a grand lady
"Moss Gown"	North Carolina (Eastern coast) plantations	Candace (also known as Moss Gown)	Stepsisters and father	Scullery maid; honesty	Gris-Gris Woman	Heroine marries the young master and is reunited with her father

people who told them. It is clear, for instance, from the discussion of Cinderella variants, that children all over the world are, and were, frequently abused, especially females.

But the differences between the stories are also revealing. Although the girls in the Cinderella stories prove their purity and win their men in a variety of ways, in the differences lie hints of the importance people place today and long ago on certain kinds of behavior. In "Yeh-Shen," the girl wins a husband because she has endured, a quality which the Chinese have always valued. In "Vassilisa the Beautiful," Vassilisa wins her husband because of her quick wit (with the help of her doll), perhaps a quality that the Russians value. Burnt Face and Moss Gown succeed in winning over their men because they are truthful, the little girls in "The Month Brothers" and "Talking Eggs" because they are kind. In "Benizara and Kakezara," Benizara wins a husband when she composes a poem, a testimony to the value Japanese place on the art of writing poetry and on beauty in general. The values of the storytellers, and therefore of the cultures from which they came, are thereby placed in relief.

After children hear stories like these, it seems appropriate for teachers to discuss the lifestyles of the people who told the tales. Most of the European tales are set in remote villages in or near dark, threatening forests, suggesting a people who are isolated in a threatening world. The Native American Cinderella, Burnt Face, lives in a tent close to nature and close to supernatural power; Moss Gown lives on a plantation in the Tidewater section of Eastern North Carolina, bringing to mind the antebellum South; and the heroine of the Creole tale "Talking Eggs" lives in rural Louisiana like many Southern blacks, on a small farm. Yeh-Shen, on the other hand, like many Hmong living near Canton even today, lives in a cave. The lifestyles suggested by the stories become vehicles for discussing the way people lived long ago.

The variants, with their reflections on the lifestyles and values of the people who first told them, are thus powerful tools for teaching. When children get acquainted with these old stories, they can take pride in their own backgrounds and learn to appreciate differences among cultures. In the process, they also learn that fairy tales are often similar to each other, that the similarities and differences are cues to the people who first told the stories. Above all, they learn that the stories are links in a never-ending chain of stories about the human condition.

REFERENCES

Christiansen, R. T. (Ed.). (1964). *Folktales of Norway*. Translated by Pat Shaw Iversen. Chicago: University of Chicago Press.

Cohen, B. (Reteller). (1990). *Lovely Vassilisa*. Illustrated by Anatoly Ivanoff. New York: Atheneum.

Coxan, M. (1893). *Cinderella: 345 variants*. London: Nutt.

Degh, L. (1969). *Folktales and society: Storytelling in a Hungarian peasant community*. Translated by E. Schossberger. Bloomington: Indiana University Press.

De La Mare, W. (1959). *Tales told again*. London: Faber.

deWit, D. (Ed.). (1979). *The talking stone: An anthology of Native American tales and legends*. New York: Greenwillow.

Diamond, D. (Reteller). (1983). *Rumpelstiltskin*. Illustrated by Donna Diamond. New York: Holiday House.

Gardner, J. (1975). *Dragon, dragon and other tales*. Illustrated by Charles Shields. New York: Knopf.

Hooks, W. H. (1978). *Moss gown*. Illustrated by Donald Carrick. New York: Clarion.

Keen, S. (1988). Stories we live by. *Psychology Today, 22*(12), 42–47.

Louie, A. (1982). *Yeh-Shen*. Illustrated by Ed Young. New York: Philomel.

Marshak, S. (1983). *The month brothers*. Translated by Thomas P. Whitney. Illustrated by Diane Stanley. New York: Morrow.

Martin, R. (1992). *The Rough-Faced Girl*. Illustrated by David Shannon. New York: Putnam.

Ness, E. (1965). *Tom Tit Tot*. Illustrated by Eveline Ness. New York: Scribner's.

Perrault, C. (1697). Histoires ou contes du temps passé, avec de moralitz. In Barchilon J. & Flinder, P. (1981). *Charles Perrault*. Boston: Twayne.

Pyle, H. (1887). *Pepper and salt, or seasoning for young people*. New York: Harper & Row.

Rooth, A. (1951). *The Cinderella cycle*. Lund, Sweden: Gleerup.

San Souci, R. (1989). *The talking eggs: A folktale from the American South*. Illustrated by Jerry Pinkney. New York: Dial.

Seki, K. (1963). *Folktales of Japan*. Translated by Robert J. Adams. Chicago: University of Chicago Press.

Steptoe, J. (1987). *Mufaro's beautiful daughters*. New York: Lothrop, Lee & Shepard.

Yearsley, M. (1968). *The folklore of fairytale*. Detroit: Singing Tree.

Zemach, H. (1973). *Duffy and the devil*. Illustrated by Margo Zemach. New York: Farrar, Straus, & Giroux.

TRY THIS

Help the children learn how fairy tales are similar by encouraging them to compare two or three tales that are alike in some way. They can compare:

1. Tales that are similar at the beginning and the end
2. Tales from different countries or regions
3. Stories with similar motifs
4. Stories with similar tale types
5. Characters: heroes, heroines, magic figures, etc.
6. Rhymes and other language
7. Illustrations
8. The tasks the characters must complete

Select from the Bibliography below two or three stories to compare one aspect of folklore; for instance, stories with similar heroes or heroines or with similar motifs. Read the stories to your class. Help the children compare the tales by constructing a matrix like the following:

Folktale Comparison Chart

Story	Rhyme	Magic figure	The task	Heroine
"Rumpelstilstkin"				
"Tom Tit Tot"				
"Duffy and the Devil"				

BIBLIOGRAPHY

Below is a bibliography of fairy tales suited for comparison. Read the stories that are grouped together to your pupils and then compare them. A matrix like the one above will help the children understand how they are similar to and different from each other.

—*G.B.*

The Adventures of Jack or Jim

Briggs, R. (1970). *Jim and the beanstalk*. New York: Coward, McCann & Geoghegan.

Cauley, L. B. (1983). *Jack and the bean stalk.* New York: Putnam.

Gag, W. (1974). *The story of Mother Twaddle and the marvelous achievements of her son, Jack.* New York: Seabury.

Haley, G. (1986). *Jack and the bean tree.* New York: Crown.

Still, J. (1977). *Jack and the wonder beans.* Illustrated by Margot Tomes. New York: Putnam.

Sleeping Beauties

Grimm, J., & Grimm, W. K. (1972). *Snow White and the seven dwarfs.* Translated by Randall Jarrell. Illustrated by Nancy Ekholm Burkert. New York: Farrar, Straus & Giroux.

Grimm, J., & Grimm, W. K. (1974). *The sleeping beauty.* Illustrated by Trina Schart Hyman. Boston: Little, Brown.

Grimm, J., & Grimm, W. K. (1975). *Thorn Rose and Sleeping Beauty.* Illustrated by Errol Le Cain. New York: Bradbury.

Grimm, J., & Grimm, W. K. (1979). *Sleeping Beauty.* Illustrated by Warwick Hutton. New York: Atheneum.

Perrault, C. (1889). Sleeping Beauty in the wood. In *The blue fairy book.* Edited by Andrew Lang. Illustrated by H. J. Ford & G. P. Jacomb Hood. pp. 54–63. New York: McGraw-Hill.

Perrault, C. (1964). Sleeping Beauty. In A. David & M. E. David (Eds.), *The twelve dancing princesses and other fairy tales.* New York: New American Library.

Transformations

Grimm, J., & Grimm, W. K. (1936). The frog prince. In *Tales from Grimm.* Translated and illustrated by Wanda Gag. New York: Coward, McCann & Geoghegan.

Crompton, A. E. (1975). *The winter wife.* Illustrated by Robert Parker. Boston: Little, Brown.

Harris, C. (1973). The prince who was taken away by salmon. In *Once more upon a totem.* Illustrated by Douglas Tait. pp. 7–62. New York: Atheneum.

Yagawa, S. (1981). *The crane wife.* Translated by Katherine Paterson. Illustrated by Suekichi Akaba. New York: Morrow.

Devils and Heroines

Grimm, J., & Grimm, W. K. (1986). *Rumpelstiltskin.* Illustrated by Paul Zelinsky. New York: Dutton.

Ness, E. (1965). *Tom Tit Tot.* New York: Scribner's.

Zemach, H. (1973). *Duffy and the devil.* Illustrated by Margot Zemach. New York: Farrar, Straus & Giroux.

Point of View

Claverie, J. (1989). *The three little pigs.* Monchaldorf, Switzerland: North-South Books.
Scieszcka, J. (1989). *The true story of the three little pigs.* Illustrated by Lane Smith. New York: Viking Penguin.

Art Work

Galdone, P. (1974). *Little Red Riding Hood.* New York: McGraw-Hill.
Goodall, J. S. (1988). *Little Red Riding Hood.* New York: Macmillan.

Changes in Tale Type or Story Structure

Gavin, B. (1984). *Chicken Licken.* Oxford: Oxford University Press.
Kellogg, S. (1985). *Chicken Little.* New York: Morrow.

CHAPTER 7

CREATING VARIANTS WITH ILLUSTRATIONS

Patricia J. Cianciolo

Dr. Cianciolo continues her discussion of folklore variants in the innovative chapter that follows. According to her, artists create variants through a variety of artistic choices that they make as they shape their picture storybook versions of fairy tales, through the way they depict characters in the story, through the scenes they choose to illustrate, and the artistic styles they use. The variants they create are as distinctive as those that come through the traditional folklore process. For teachers their variants can be a window of opportunity for teaching. For the children the pictures can be an early experience with fine art.

Most people think of folktale variants as two or more stories differing in motifs, the smallest story elements in a plot. An example is "Cinderella." In some versions ("Cinderella"), a fairy godmother saves her, in others ("Yeh-Shen") a fish protects her, in still others ("Tattercoats") a gooseherder rescues the heroine. Because a different magical object is used, each story is somewhat different from other versions.

The folklorist Stith Thompson used motifs to analyze stories at a time when few picture storybooks of folktales existed. Today, however, because many different picture book versions of fairy tales are available, we have variant forms even when the story line is identical to that of other tales. To help you understand more fully what I mean, let us first review some basic principles about book illustrations.

BOOK ILLUSTRATIONS AS ART

Strictly speaking, one cannot separate words and illustrations when evaluating or analyzing illustrations in a picture book or illustrated book version of folktale retellings. Each form of expression (word and picture) creates conditions of dependence and interdependence so that the full meaning of any book illustration can only be revealed within the context of the two elements. Furthermore, a book of illustrations together amounts to far more than a book would if it contained a single picture, even though, in and of itself, an individual picture is beautiful and appears to be as complete and comprehensive a work of art as any gallery painting could be. When viewed as an illustration designed to express the literary elements voiced in a tale, the perspective of the picture changes. The picture deepens and broadens in mood, rhythm, design, and meaning, creating a special gestalt.

The art that is produced goes far beyond a photographic accuracy to create an illusion. What is expressed is a selective interpretation, an illusion rather than a miniature reality (Sontag, pp. 4–7). Works of art—book art or any other form of art—are not mirror reflections of reality. Nor is there any real distinction between art and illustration. The most significant point to consider when examining a book illustration (or gallery painting, sketch, or sculpture figure) is the *illusion* in art.

Because the "essence of art is not imitation but expression" (Gombrich, p. 356), most modern artists interpret ideas and concepts through the medium used (woodblock print, watercolor, or grease pencil) and within range of the tones the medium will yield. The "personal accent" inherent in the expression of these ideas and concepts is revealed in unique qualities of distribution, sequence, and relationships of the artist's movements and shapes.

The attitude shared by artists about what constitutes artistic expression explains clearly why we find such diversity in picture books and illustrated books. Even when different artists use the identical text to illustrate their pictures, they tell different stories. Folktales have been told without illustrations as long as humans have used language to communicate their ideas, values, and creative imaginings. But once illustrations exist, they inevitably change the story. Book artists, many of whom are creators of sophisticated pictures, interpret the meanings of words in specific ways. Each picture offers the reader something definite and new, perhaps more detailed and interesting than the words that tell the story.

Some people say that pictures limit the reader's imagination and the range of possible meanings one brings to words because they shape images and impose them on the reader. But then, so do words. Perry Nodelman (1984), author of the article "How Picture Books Work," reminds us that "the only safe alternative (to shaping an image) is utterly blank pages," (p. 10) and that leads to no story at all. Admittedly, pictures in folktale retellings (or any other kind of literature) can to some extent limit one's response to words. But a book artist can also tell his/her part of the story by creating visuals that sharpen the eyes, mind, and feelings of the viewer.

The visual (graphic) artist decides by selective interpretation to include in his/her illustrations only certain aspects of the human experience addressed in the story, as well as reality in general. Because each book artist differs in use of color, line, shading, space, and the way an episode is depicted, he/she can convey a special individuality like that seen in fingerprints and voice prints. The result is that when a number of book artists create picture book versions of the same story, each one creates a picture book variation of that story.

PICTURE BOOK VARIANTS

The legend of the "Pied Piper of Hamelin" is a well-known example of a fairy tale told many times in prose and poetry. When three book artists, Kate Greenaway, C. Walter Hodges, and Anatoly Ivanov, retold Robert Browning's version of the story, they created three variants of the story about the man who piped the village free of rats and children after the town council refused to pay him for getting rid of rats. Tony Ross, on the other hand, used his own prose and his own expressionistic cartoonlike illustrations to retell a variant of the legend. Let us see how each artist made use of these aspects of the story.

Each of these book artists' visual retelling is decidedly different from the others, even though the text by Robert Browning is essentially the same. In every book each artist employs a different style of art and different media (collage, gouache, water color, pastels, ink, and so on) or the same medium in a different manner. But more important, each artist highlights different details, and grants different personality traits and physical characteristics to the piper, the town's leaders, the population of Hamelin, and the rats that plagued the town.

Evidence of how each book artist creates a variant of this legend through his/her illustrations becomes apparent as one examines how each makes use of the cover pictures, endpapers, title pages, the main character (the piper), and specific episodes.

Cover Pictures

Anatoly Ivanov's (Browning, 1986) front cover is suggestive of (but not at all like) the stained glass window that was installed in the Market Church in Hamelin, Germany, around the year 1300, to commemorate 130 children and a flute-playing stranger who disappeared on June 16, 1284. Ivanov's window, consisting of three parts, depicts a vengeful-looking piper playing the fife, followed on the left by gleeful children. Townspeople standing on the right, watching all this occur, are obviously befuddled and powerless to prevent it. From a window of the church steeple, at the far left corner of the back cover, one sees the rooftops of this medieval town. The intense black background on the cover of this picture book seems quite appropriate for the ominous events in the legend.

Tony Ross (1977) has two pictures on his cover: The front cover picture shows a rather foppish piper enchanting a bewhiskered rat dancing on the piper's knee. The back cover picture shows the lame boy pulling his wooden toy as he walks through the deserted town, bored and lonely. Left behind because he was unable to keep up with his playmates as they followed the piper around the mountain path, through the temporary portal, to the beautiful and scenic land of Transylvania, the boy is the only remaining child in the town of Hamelin.

Kate Greenaway (Browning, 1888), whose naive, decorative, tidy watercolor pictures always focus on the bright side of life, shows the same serene pastoral scene on the front and back covers of her picture book: Fairylike and elfin children prance around a flower-laden tree, and at the shore of the river, the piper, sitting nearby, plays his pipe and is surrounded by children clinging to him and sitting at his feet among the flowers, birds, and cats. They obviously are awed by and enchanted with the piper.

The cover picture on C. Walter Hodges's (Browning, 1971) picture book is an expressionistic, line-and-wash double-page spread showing the piper playing his pipe as the rats, attracted and charmed by his music, gather in front of him; curious and happy children follow him through the winding streets of this medieval town.

Endpapers and Title Pages

The endpapers and title pages are used in various ways by book artists to tell their stories. One artist might use them to establish the mood or to reiterate the theme of the story. Another might use the front endpaper and/or title page to begin the story and the back endpapers to conclude the telling of the tale. Still another might use them as vehicles to identify or summarize the major events of the tale.

Anatoly Ivanov presents on his title page a musical pipe bedecked with a gaudy scarf. Resting on the pipe is an old, dilapidated crest consisting of four equal parts, each representing four major episodes of this legend. Moving from left to right, starting at the top of the crest, one sees a huge rat and a medieval village; on the bottom half on the left side is a white rose in a background of blood red (symbolizing innocent children plucked from their loving parents and sacrificed because the town's leaders refused to pay their debts to the piper?); on the bottom right side is the piper playing his pipe.

Kate Greenaway depicts a crest, too, but it is placed on the endpaper instead of the title page. The crest, represented four times on the front and back endpapers, depicts what was probably the coat of arms of the Hanover royal family—lions holding a stylized H, topped with medieval castles. A rat is placed at each corner of the framed picture, and a ribbon-bedecked musical pipe frames the top half of each of Greenaway's endpapers.

The back and front endpapers in Tony Ross's picture book offer the same panoramic view of the medieval town surrounded with a moat and high brick wall, and the children following the piper out of town. Encircled at the top and right hand corner of the picture is Duke Klaus's medieval castle. (According to Ross's text, Klaus, one of the 130 children who followed the piper out of Hamelin to Transylvania, eventually was made a duke.) At the bottom of the picture, in the corner at the left is the duke's crest. Ross spoofs the Hanover crest here: Instead of the H in the center he shows a cross-eyed, frowning, highly stylized lion; a bewhiskered rat is positioned on each side of the crest, instead of lions. His title page depicts the piper prancing through the woods as he plays his musical pipe.

The picture on Kate Greenaway's title page depicts a boy and girl in pursuit of something. Later we know that it is the piper the children are happily running after, and they are leaving Hamelin never to be seen again. Facing the title page is the same picture that is on the cover. Again, Greenaway emphasizes the happiness that the piper brought to the children in the town of Hamelin, instead of the alarm and dismay brought to the parents.

C. Walter Hodges has no pictures on his endpapers. No picture appears on the title page, either; but facing it is an expressionistic interpretation of an impish-looking piper.

Episodes

One way to see quite clearly how variants occur in the pictorial retelling of a folktale (or any other kind of story, for that matter) is to notice how book artists concentrate on the episodes that make up the tale. When making the illustrations for a picture book version of a tale, the artist must show each of these episodes as complete within itself. Thus, as one moves from page to page of the picture book, one sees a sequence of isolated episodes. The task of the illustrator is not to show how one moment is related to the next; the text does that. The illustrator's task is to create a sequence of pictures containing details that make the reader consider specifics about the action; the place, and/or the characters' feelings and emotions important in each episode are to be highlighted. How each book artist illustrates the major episodes inevitably varies from the way other book artists illustrate them if they happen to choose to provide pictures for the same episode in their retellings.

Each of the five book artists interprets the entrance of the Pied Piper to Hamelin and the children following him out. To increase his readers' interest and arouse curiosity, C. Walter Hodges first shows the obese, pompous, and rather simple councillors looking anxiously at the closed chamber door. Upon turning the page we find the piper in the chamber, the door ajar (Figure 7.1). He looks like an Elizabethan clown, flamboyant and self-assured.

Anatoly Ivanov uses much the same storytelling technique as C. Walter Hodges. On one double-page spread the robust Lower Saxony councilmen appear wide-eyed and frightened when the piper taps at the door. When one turns the page, one sees a tall, weatherbeaten, suntanned traveler dressed in a long, loose-fitting, gaudy, red and yellow cloak, and bowing with gracefulness and flourish, no doubt, to the men shown on the previous page (Figure 7.2). The jeweled pins on his soft leather boots and scarf and the high-quality musical pipe that is in impeccable condition tell the reader that the piper is far from impoverished.

Kate Greenaway presents the piper as a humble, self-effacing young peasant (Figure 7.3). He apparently halted as he entered the chamber, for he is shown standing barely one step beyond the doorway. Greenaway does not show the reader how the council members respond to this stranger's tap on the chamber door or their first glimpse of him. The image of the piper she presents is that of a young man too refined and delicate to be true, especially when we learn later in the story that he acts with vengeance after the council refuses to pay him the sum they promised.

In contrast, Tony Ross shows a craggy and rugged piper who, having entered the chamber without being noticed by the council, bows in mockery to the mayor and the council (all elder statesmen), who are holding their meeting standing on top of the table, huddled together because they are afraid of the grotesque rats that surround them on the floor below (Figure 7.4).

Let us glance at how each book artist shows the children following the piper out of Hamelin. Notice how the personality of each piper is reflected in the children. Tony Ross shows the children prancing and foppish like the piper. Anatoly Ivanov's children are as graceful and as showy as the worldwise piper they are following. Kate Greenaway's children seem as sweet and naive as their leader, in contrast to the impish children and piper depicted by C. Walter Hodges.

The artists differ in the number of pictures they created to tell their story. Schwarz, Ivanov, and Ross were true to the style of the folktale. They told their stories without digressions, each using a distinctive picture style

Figure 7.1   Walter Hodges' Pied Piper

and a fairly small number of pictures for each of their retellings. Anatoly Ivanov created 15 double-page spreads plus one single-page picture for his picture-book retelling, all done with a gouache in strong colors, realistic style, and detail. A definite rhythm is readily apparent in Ivanov's illustrations as the reader moves from page to page; one moves easily from the panoramic view of the medieval town to a closer view of the townspeople plagued by rats, to a still closer view of the perplexed council members, and

Figure 7.2 Anatoly Ivanov's Pied Piper

then to the piper himself. The reader is gradually moved again to more distant views until he sees a panoramic view of the children following the piper. The story ends with a close-up of a book, its covers closed upon a red rose, symbolizing faithfulness, one of the themes of this story. The narrator's closing words, "If we've promised them aught, let us keep our promise!" are printed directly above the illustration. Tony Ross made 17 line-and-wash expressionistic, cartoon styled drawings for his picture book version of the Pied Piper, seven double-page spreads, six full-page pictures, and four pictures that cover about one half of each page.

C. Walter Hodges and Kate Greenaway strayed from folktale style, for their retellings included a proliferation of illustrations and digressions. C. Walter Hodges made 27 sophisticated expressionistic pictures with ink, pas-

Figure 7.3   Kate Greenaway's Pied Piper

tels, and watercolor wash; two are double-page spreads. Kate Greenaway made 36 watercolor pictures, each framed with a thin black line. Even the three double-page spreads are broken up by these frames. Most of her pictures depict one or two or small groups of people lacking body color and

Figure 7.4 Tony Ross' Pied Piper

clad in Victorian-styled clothes. The children are dainty, ethereal, charming, and innocent, living not in 13th-century Hamelin, when the incidents described in this tale were said to have occurred, but in a decidedly bucolic world vaguely adorned with idyllic trappings "detached from period and place." (Meyer, p. 109)

CONCLUSION

In this way, through pictures, five book artists each created a variant for the well-known legend "The Pied Piper of Hamelin." Fascinating as the pictures are to consider in and of themselves, there are several basic implications in all this for the book selector, too.

First, if we introduce many visual interpretations or picture-book versions of the same story to our students, especially folktales and classics, we open the children to a broad set of experiences, and we shortchange them indeed if we provide only one version. Each set of pictures, each visual variant, strongly influences the reader's response to the tale. The specific images pictures offer *limit* or *impose* the information that the reader may glean from the verbal version of the story; or a set of pictures may also *amplify* the information that most readers would bring to these words. They introduce new and decidedly different ideas from what the readers would, or even could, bring to words. Think how one's horizons can be extended imaginatively and factually by reading beautifully crafted picture-book variants of folktales or any other stories, for that matter.

Second, an important reason for making more than one picture-book version of the same stories is that the exposure to diverse art styles used to illustrate stories that children understand and enjoy helps them to be more accepting, perhaps even more appreciative, of diversity in artistic expression everywhere—in homes and art galleries as well as in books. Ultimately, this appreciation may help children be more discriminating. They may find the joy and beauty in the personal, handmade visual statements of reality created by artists through selective interpretation and talented handling of media and style.

Third, by exposure to many in the process, children may recognize that one person's preference for a style of art may differ from another's. That is as it should be, for conformity in the realm of art (be it graphic art and/or literary art) or politics or religion is not a virtue but a vice.

REFERENCES

Browning, R. (1971). *The pied piper of Hamelin*. Illustrated by C. Walter Hodges. New York: Coward, McCann & Geoghegan.

Browning, R. (1986). *The pied piper of Hamelin*. Illustrated by Anatoly Ivanov. New York: Lothrop, Lee & Shepard.

Browning, R. (1888). *The pied piper of Hamelin*. Illustrated by Kate Greenaway. New York: Warne.

Nodelman, P. (1984). How picture books work. In H. Darling and P. Neumeyer (Eds.), *Image and maker* (pp. 1–10). La Jolla, CA: Green Tiger.

Ross, T. (Reteller). (1977). *The pied piper of Hamelin.* Illustrated by Tony Ross. New York: Lothrop, Lee & Shepard.

BIBLIOGRAPHY

Gombrich, E. H. (1969). *Art and illusion: A study of the psychology of pictorial representation.* Princeton: Princeton University Press.

Meyer, S. E. (1983). *A treasury of the great children's book illustrators.* New York: Abrams.

Shulevitz, U. (August, 1969). Caldecott acceptance. *Horn Book,* pp. 385–388.

Sontag, S. (1977). *On photography.* New York: Farrar, Straus & Giroux.

TRY THIS

Read several variants of "The Pied Piper of Hamelin" (see Chapter 7 references) with your class. Before starting, point out that although the stories are often similar, the artists make the stories different through their treatment of

1. The cover pictures
2. The endpapers
3. The title pages
4. Episodes
5. The main characters

Ask the group to create their own books of variants.

—G.B.

CHAPTER 8

❀ Fairy tales belong in the CLASSROOM

Bette Bosma

It is probably safe to say that most elementary school teachers make use of fairy tales in some way in their classes. They may read favorite tales like "The Three Billy Goats Gruff" or tell others like "Ali Baba and the Forty Thieves." Many teachers help children to act out favorites or write "fractured" fairy tales. Whatever teachers do, it is possible that they may miss some teaching opportunities.

In this chapter, Professor Bosma describes a number of fresh ideas for teaching fairy tales. Although some teachers may have tried a few of her suggestions on their own, they will surely find others that they have not considered. Professor Bosma describes ways of exploring the rhythmic language of fairy tales and makes suggestions for clarifying the meanings of new words. She suggests lively approaches to teaching story structure, as well as unique methods for story mapping, visual arts, and writing. She also discusses ways to take advantage of commonplace fairy tale features like stereotypes and motifs.

Young readers delight in stories that create a world of wonder. The first and most important reason for including fairy tales in the classroom is enjoyment. When the teacher and children enjoy the stories together, they develop a comfortable camaraderie in the classroom. Repeated reading and responding to the stories extends that enjoyment and develops lifelong appreciation of the tales. A rich exposure to fairy tales stretches creative energies beyond everyday living and encourages children to dream.

Ross-Ramon (1980) found in his study of young children and folktales that the language and tales of kings, trolls, elves, and witches are much closer to the actuality of children's play than are many modern realistic stories. Realistic stories mirror life for a small segment of readers who have experienced that slice of life. Folktales, on the other hand, offer a broad dimension of human experience through characters who are symbols of good or evil, wisdom or foolishness, strength or weakness.

Iona and Peter Opie (1974) define a fairy tale as an unbelievable tale that includes an enchantment or a supernatural element that is clearly imaginary. It does not necessarily contain fairies. Such stories are also referred to as household tales or wonder tales, and include entertaining stories of people's adventures with the supernatural. Children relate to the wishes, dreams, and hopes of the fairy-tale characters and find comfort in the fantastical solutions to problems.

A traditional fairy tale is a work of art that passes from one generation to another in the telling. Children's literature includes beautifully illustrated and retold fairy tales that belong in the classroom. This chapter presents ideas to help teachers introduce these books and enhance children's experiences with the tales.

FAIRY TALES AND LANGUAGE LEARNING

Many children hear traditional literature for the first time at school. The introduction to the fairy tale in any grade is with a teacher expressively telling or reading the story aloud. Fairy tales are first of all meant to be enjoyed. Appreciation of the tales is added to enjoyment when teachers use strategies to facilitate language encounters, awareness of story structure, and creative responses to the stories.

Language Encounters Throughout the Grades

The rhythmic, predictable language of the fairy tale gives the young child a comfortable feeling when listening to the stories. The fairy tale should be told dramatically and directly, with vivid words that can create images.

Telling the story frees the teacher to observe the listeners and note the degree of active involvement each one demonstrates. The teacher can encourage active listening by asking predictive questions and stopping to let the children to join in the rhythmic lines.

I would urge every teacher to memorize and practice at least one tale. It is not necessary to reproduce the story word for word, but care should be given to use the literary, predictable language that is characteristic of the traditional story. Children in older grades can learn from the teacher's model and become storytellers themselves. This will require careful planning, allowing time to study the components of the story and the language patterns and to practice with a partner. A good test of the children's skill would be for them to perform their story in a primary class. *Handbook for Storytellers* (Bauer, 1977) offers practical suggestions and encouragement for the beginning storyteller.

Reading the story allows the teacher to share the artist's imaginative interpretation of the tale. When teachers read from a profusely illustrated edition such as *Rumpelstiltskin,* beautifully retold and painted by Paul Zelinsky (1986), they should sit or stand at an angle to the children and display the pictures while reading. Young children cannot be expected to make visual images of objects such as castles, kings and queens, and giants until they have seen some representations. By seeing versions of the same story illustrated by different artists, the children can see for themselves that fairy-tale settings can be pictured in a variety of ways. After close scrutiny of these skillfully illustrated tales, the children will be ready to produce their own visual impressions of characters, settings, and actions.

An important objective of these experiences is to help children become aware of language. Fairy tales such as *The Fisherman and His Wife, Jack and the Beanstalk, The Elves and the Shoemaker,* and *The Fool of the World and the Flying Ship* contain repetitive and cumulative patterns, and sometimes use synonyms or variations of a phrase. The following lesson can be adapted for any story that includes such variations of pattern.

LESSON PLAN LANGUAGE ENCOUNTERS

LESSON OBJECTIVE: To help children learn that different words can give the same message.

Throughout such a close scrutiny of the language, one must be sure to maintain the integrity of the story, allowing the language study to be an exploratory exchange of ideas rather than an imposed requirement. Therefore, this lesson is intended as a group oral discussion rather than an individual writing assignment.

MATERIALS: *The Fool of the World and the Flying Ship* (Ransome, 1968)—multiple copies, if possible, but one per pupil is not necessary; chart paper; and markers.

PROCEDURE: (for use with six to eight children)

1. Before reading the story, ask the children why someone would be called the "fool of the world." Ask them to decide while they are listening (or reading to themselves) if the main character is a fool and why he got that name.
2. Read the story to the group, or guide the children as they read silently.
3. After reading, allow time for the children to respond to the story. Ask them if he was really a fool.

4. Look back into the story for phrases that establish the rhythm of the story through repetition. Chart the varieties of one basic response. For example, whenever Fool met someone he would say

> "Good-day to you, uncle."
> "Good health to you, uncle."

His invitation would be

> Take your place in the ship with me
> Take your seat with us
> There's a place for you with us
> There's a place here for you too

5. Elicit from the children the commands from the Czar that told you he was giving the Fool another task. Chart similar commands:

> Go to the Fool and tell him . . .
> Go to the captain of the flying ship and give him . . . this message
> Tell the Fool
> Tell the fellow

Ask what Listener did. Chart the words used to describe this.

6. Ask the reader, "How do these statements help you anticipate what is going to happen next?"

AWARENESS OF STORY STRUCTURE

The traditional storyteller followed literary conventions that play an important role in developing a child's sense of story. The structure of fairy tales follows predictably: a conventional opening (often "Once upon a time"), a setting, introductions to characters, an initiating event, a problem, attempts to solve the problem, and a resolution.

Since not every child understands the structure of fairy tales equally well, the teacher may want to find out how well individual children understand structure. A lesson in predicting the elements of the story will help both the teacher and the child to discover their story expectations. Children who hear and read many traditional tales gain structural insights that help develop their intuitive ability to understand narration. Knowing how a piece of writing unfolds lifts the reader from viewing a book as a succession of words, or isolated sentences, to seeing it as an exciting story evolving from a natural flow of language.

Before teaching the lesson described below, a teacher should read Jane Yolen's (1986) version of *Sleeping Beauty* to the class. The lesson includes reading Jane Yolen's invented fairy tale, *Sleeping Ugly* (1981).

The Sleeping Beauty as retold by Jane Yolen begins with "Once upon a time there lived a King and Queen who wanted only one thing—to have a child" (p. 1).

That problem is quickly solved, but a more complex problem follows and the story proceeds with elements typically found in the story structure of fairy tales.

LESSON PLAN STORY STRUCTURE

LESSON OBJECTIVE: To elicit predictions from the listeners that reveal their expectations for fairy tales.

MATERIALS: *Sleeping Ugly,* a modern fairy tale written by Jane Yolen; chart paper; and markers.

PROCEDURE: Before reading the book, ask the class what they expect to find in a fairy tale.

1. Record children's responses on chart. Encourage them by asking probing questions such as, "If someone falls asleep, how long do they usually sleep? How many wishes will there be? Who solves the problem?"
2. Read the story, enjoying the play on words and humorous changes in the tale.
3. Ask, "Does *Sleeping Ugly* follow the traditional fairy tale pattern?" Now complete the chart. Compare how the invented story followed fairy tale tradition or was different from it.

A group of third and fourth graders gave the responses shown on the chart in Table 8.1.

With this approach, the story is being read primarily for enjoyment, but when children discuss the story structure they also develop an appreciation of the tale.

The Baba Yaga adventures from Russia fit the home-adventure-home pattern because the wicked witch cannot win against truth, love, and human kindness, and virtuous children escape from her magic. To Russian children, Baba Yaga is a household name. *Anna and the Seven Swans* as retold by Maida Silverman (1984) is one of the less complicated plots and a good tale for modeling the home-adventure-home plot pattern. Other books to read and chart are *Baba Yaga* retold by Ernest Small (1966) and "Vasilisa the Fair" from *The Firebird* by Boris Zvorykin (1978).

Table 8.1 A comparison chart of a group of third and fourth graders' responses to a traditional and non-traditional fairy-tale

Before reading A *traditional* fairy tale	After reading Jane Yolen's *Sleeping Ugly*
Begins with "Once upon a time"	Begins with "Once upon a time"
About beauty	
Has princess, king, queen	Has princess, prince
Prince rescues the princess	Prince rescues Jane
Three wishes	Three wishes
It lasts 100 years if someone sleeps	Princess sleeps forever
Has a fairy or a witch	Has both fairy and witch

Ends with "Lived happily
  ever after"
	Ends with "Lived happily
	  ever after"

IMAGINARY KINGDOMS

Imagination can help children understand reality. Geographic terms used in Social Studies come into sharp focus when children can relate real and make-believe.

The fifth-grade class of Nancy Hardee in Holland, Michigan, was engaged in a project that integrated Social Studies and literature. Their Social Studies curriculum included many geographical terms. Mrs. Hardee introduced these terms by identifying various places on maps and playing games to help the children gain familiarity with the terms. The children gained working knowledge of the terms when they designed imaginary countries, or kingdoms, in which they used all of the geographical terms. They invented sites such as Delight Bay and Magic Peninsula.

Mrs. Hardee guided the children in observing artists' impressions of geographic locations. The children listened to the stories, and then studied the illustrations, in the following books:

> *The Sleeping Beauty,* retold by Jane Yolen, illustrated by Ruth Sanderson.
>
> *Mufaro's Beautiful Daughters,* retold and illustrated by John Steptoe.
>
> *Rumpelstiltskin,* retold and illustrated by Paul Zelinsky.
>
> *The Twelve Dancing Princesses,* retold by Janet Lunn, illustrated by Laszlo Gal.
>
> *Snow-White and the Seven Dwarfs,* retold by Randall Jarrell, illustrated by Nancy Burkert.
>
> *Tattercoats,* retold by Flora Annie Steele, illustrated by Diane Goode.

After studying the illustrations of variants of *Sleeping Beauty, Snow White, Rapunzel,* and *Rumpelstiltskin,* the children began to fantasize a magical kingdom of their own. They viewed and compared the artists' versions with pictures and descriptions of existing castles and countrysides in England and Germany. Included was Neuschwanstein Castle near Fussen, Germany, which was the inspiration for the Disney World castle.

When the children were ready to plan their own countries, they drew their design on paper with pencils. When they were satisfied with their plan, the children fashioned their country out of "Great Stuff," a material similar to play dough, forming three-dimensional maps on boards. (See Figure 8.1 for the Great Stuff recipe.)

The children wrote a key to identify all of the geographical terms and they used a variety of techniques in doing this. Some used flags on toothpicks, others used colored dots, and still others used numbers. Afterwards, they wrote stories telling of the adventures of kings and queens, princes and princesses, and peasants in the imaginary lands. They shared their stories and displayed their kingdoms by inviting other classes, friends, and family to visit their classroom.

BUILDING APPRECIATION FOR FAIRY TALES

True appreciation of traditional literature is developed by careful and clear guidance in critical thinking and reading. Extensive reading of authentic literary versions of fairy tales leads the reader to recognize the dignity, beauty, and symbolism of the stories as well as the harshness and glimpses of realism they contain. A critical study includes understanding the characters, comparing and contrasting variants of the tales from different lands, exploring the relationship of the culture of the people to the elements found in the stories, comparing and evaluating illustrations in variants of the same tale, studying fairy tale motifs and the various ways in which they are interpreted by different storytellers.

Variants of tales and the artwork of the literature are discussed in other chapters in this book. This chapter will include ideas for understanding fairy-tale characters, a study of fairy tales and culture, and a study of fairy-tale motifs.

Stereotypes in Fairy Tales

Fairy-tale characters are often stereotypical and depicted as symbols of good or evil, wise or foolish, powerful or weak (Bosma, 1992). Rather than deplore this stereotyping, the teacher can use it to help children understand

GREAT STUFF

| 2 cups table salt | 1 cup corn starch |
| 2/3 cup water | 1/2 cup cold water |

Mix salt and 2/3 cup water in a saucepan over low heat, stirring for about 3 minutes. Remove from heat. Immediately mix cornstarch and 1/2 cup cold water, then add all at once to salt and water mixture. Stir quickly to combine. Mixture should thicken to consistency of stiff dough. If it doesn't, place pan over low heat for about 1 minute. Put mixture on work surface and knead as you would dough, to form smooth pliable mass.

> *Double Batch:* double all ingredients, follow directions given above except keep pan over heat when adding corn starch and water to hot salt mixture.

> *To color:* food colors or tempera paint may be added while heating.

When completed and GREAT STUFF is in one large ball, be sure to wrap in plastic or keep in airtight container.

Objects made from GREAT STUFF dry in about 36 hours or 30–60 minutes in an oven set at 350°F.

Figure 8.1   Recipe for map construction

the kinds of stereotypes that exist in society. Critical reading skills help readers foster the ability to cope with life. The thoughtful reader develops a standard against which judgments can be made, rather than an adherence to stereotypical beliefs or hasty judgments.

Psychologist Bruno Bettelheim (1976) claims that stereotypical, one-dimensional figures help young children to sort out their feelings toward real-life persons who have conflicting and complex character traits. The moral tales represent justice, and the violence occurs in an imaginary land. Older children are able to interpret the symbolism in fairy tales within the limits of their own life experiences.

Some persons object to the princess image as perpetuating a view of the helpless female. However, if the reader studied authentic translations of the tales of each country, rather than the romanticized Disney versions, she or he would recognize that the female is depicted as hardy and self-reliant in such tales. Russian heroines such as Vasilisa the Fair, Anna, and Marya are all shrewd, persevering young women who follow wishes with proper action in order to attain results. Few fairy-tale women stand helplessly by without contributing to resolving problems. Sleeping Beauty, who was an undeserving victim of evil, was truthful, merry, modest, and wise, in addition to being beautiful. Beauty chose to go with the Beast so that her family could have a better life (Mayer, 1978). Mistakes the heroines made caused them great hardship, which they persisted in overcoming.

The inventiveness of Cinderella is apparent in the German "Cinderella," the English "Tattercoats," the Chinese "Yeh-Shen," Vietnam's "Tam," Russia's "Vasilisa," as well as the nameless Native American Cinderella and the Zuni "Turkey Girl." Jane Yolen (1977) claims that

> the mass market American "Cinderellas" have presented the majority of American children with the wrong dream. They offer the passive princess, the "insipid beauty waiting . . . for Prince Charming," . . . and the magic of the old tales has been falsified, the true meaning lost. . . . (p. 27)

A comparison of the heroes and heroines of the tales should be directed toward understanding the characters through their actions and their responses to the hardships they endure. Fairy tales represent the fulfillment of human desires; in such tales we are secure in the knowledge that love, kindness, and truth will prevail and that hate and wickedness will be punished. The folk who retold these stories over and over were teaching their children morality and warning them against evil. The magical power in the fairy tales is limited and does not change the hearts of the characters.

Fairy Tales and Culture

Children easily accept the fairy tale as a symbolic interpretation of life in an imaginary land. They can also be guided toward recognizing the distinctive traits of other cultures by reflecting on specific characteristics of the tales as retold within those cultures. When children in intermediate grades or middle school study countries of the world or Native Americans, folktales play an important role in understanding the culture of the people studied.

Joseph Campbell (1985), an acclaimed authority on mythology, attributed the origin of folklore to the cottage, the castle, and the convent. German fairy tales appear to derive from the cottage; most of the Grimm translations are set in the Black Forest area and reflect the heavy morality of the peasantry. They believed that evil should be punished and good rewarded. The French tales, written down by Perrault, were lighter in mood, with an emphasis on extolling virtue rather than warning against evil. The castle is pictured in a friendlier style than in German tales. Norwegian stories contain undertones of realism and folk humor of the rural life, centered in family farms, where stories were told and retold in the endless, housebound winter evenings. The Norwegians linked their royalty to animals and filled their forests with magical people. Russian fairy tales contain complex adventures, the continual quest of the Russian peasant's dreams. They depict palaces filled with magic and splendor. Native American tales reveal the oneness of the people with the earth and all aspects of nature.

The reflective reader or listener, upon second or third reading of the tales, can find evidence of the characteristics cited above. A group discussion is an important means of verifying the reader's findings and comparing impressions with other students whose opinions will vary with their backgrounds. Older children can discuss the complexity of good and evil in real life versus the polarization of good and evil depicted in fairy tales. (Additional information concerning tales of specific countries is available from the Pantheon Fairy Tale and Folklore Library, Pantheon Books, New York City, a collection written for adult readers. The foreward of each volume gives cultural information about the tale.)

Motifs in Fairy Tales

A motif is an element or unit of action in a story. Stith Thompson (1932) prepared a 20-volume motif-index of folk literature that has been accepted by folklorists around the world for classifying folktales. Margaret Read MacDonald (1982) classified the motifs that appear in tales retold for children following the Stith Thompson index. Introducing the reader to motifs not only leads to a deeper understanding of the stories, but also helps the reader to see how widespread certain traits are throughout the world. In Table 8.2 representative motifs are listed using the Stith Thompson Motif-Index and examples of fairy tales that contain each motif. Many tales contain more than one motif. For example, *Tattercoats* (Steele, 1962), a British version of Cinderella, includes a least four motifs: transformation of an animal into a person, magic objects, a cruel grandfather, escape and pursuit.

A close scrutiny of the magic of the fairy tale helps the reader to ponder and elaborate on questions such as: does the magic of fairy tales change a heart or the state of the world? If not, how does the magic work to change outward conditions? Does the magic work toward rewarding good or punishing evil? How does it do that? Find evidence for each of the answers in specific tales. For example, in *Beauty and the Beast* (Mayer, 1978) the youngest daughter was the only family member who was unselfish and lov-

Table 8.2 Motifs common to versions of fairy-tales
written for children

Sample motif	Stith-Thompson index number	Title of tale	Country or culture of variant
Magic	DO 2199		
Transformation	DO-699		
Man to animal	D100	*Snow White, Red Rose*	England
Man to bird	D150	*Six Swans*	Germany
Man to frog	D195	*Black Heart of Indri*	China
Animal to person	D300	*East of the Sun, West of the Moon*	Norway
Object to object	D450	*Tattercoats* (goose feathers)	England
		Cinderella (pumpkin)	France
Magic object	D800–D1699		
Paintbrush	D1300	*Liang and The Magic Paintbrush*	China
Cooking pot (magic mill)	D1601	*Strega Nona*	Italy
		Salt	Russia
Table cloth	D861	*Lad Who Went to North Wind*	Norway
		Jack Tales	United States (Appalachia)
Lamp	D871	*Aladdin*	Arabia
Marvels	F0-1099		
Extraordinary powers	F600-F699	*Six Chinese Brothers*	China
		Long, Broad, and Quick Eye	S.E.
Remarkable persons	F500–F599	*Inch Boy*	Japan
		Thumbelina	England
		Tom Thumb	Germany
Extraordinary occurrences	F900–F1099	*Red Riding Hood*	Germany
		Twelve Dancing Princesses	Germany
Fools' quests	J1700–J2749		
Absurd disregard for facts		*The Three Sillies*	England
		Fool of the World and a Flying Ship	Russia
Tests of prowess			
Quests	H1200–H1399	*The Firebird*	Russia
		The Golden Phoenix	French Canada

ing enough to go with the beast and thus save her father. The magical transformation changed the prince's appearance, but not his character. The enchantment was a punishment for selfish actions, which was lifted through love.

Other motifs lead to comparison. To guide critical thinking, the comparison should follow three steps. First, the reader identifies the motif, such as a remarkable person, in tales from various countries. Second, the reader compares the way the remarkable people are portrayed. Third, the reader evaluates the tales by explaining what one knows and learns about the cultures of different countries from such motif variations. For example, comparing two tales with similar characters, *Inch Boy* (Morimoto, 1984) from Japan and *Tom Thumb* (Grimm, 1973) from England, demonstrates cultural differences in religion and in the ambitions of the small, noble person.

The magic motif in fairy tales takes the form of either magical objects or transformation. Both kinds of magic are worth exploring by intermediate-grade readers. Children of the 1990s are intrigued with transformers as toys. This curiosity can be extended to transformation tales, in which a human changes into an animal or bird, or an animal or bird changes into a human; sometimes they return to their original form, but often they keep the new form. Generally, the reason for the change is a reward or punishment related to their attitude about life or some good or evil they have done. A comparison study of transformation tales from various countries reveals similarities and differences. Children can discuss the ways in which the stories are the same or different. What does the story tell us about how the people think, or about the environment in which they live?

Marlene Fales, a teacher in Jenison, Michigan, studied transformation tales with her fifth graders. She began the project by leading the students in a discussion of the word "transformation," and they brainstormed examples of transformer toys and natural transformations such as caterpillar into butterfly. Then she read *East of the Sun, West of the Moon* (Hague, 1980) to the entire class. Mrs. Fales reported, "The students paid rapt attention to my reading of the tale, enjoying the characters and the beautiful descriptions."

After reading the story, she helped the students analyze and interpret it, using the chart in Figure 8.2. She used a transparency of the sheet to model responses as they worked through each question together.

The next day, Mrs. Fales presented one of her reading groups with a tub of fairy tales with a transformation motif, a list of the tales, analysis sheets, and folders in which to keep their sheets. They reviewed the steps to use in the analysis task to be sure that the students understood what was expected of them, and they set to work.

The books on their list included *The Seven Ravens, The Six Swans, The Frog Prince, Beauty and the Beast,* and *Jorinda and Joringel* from Germany; "Master Frog" in *The Brocaded Slipper* from Vietnam; "The Moss-Green Princess" in *Black Fairy Tales* from Swaziland, Africa; *The Crane Wife* from Japan; *East of the Sun, West of the Moon* from Norway; *Ring in the Prairie* and "The Prince Who Was Taken Away by the Salmon" in *Once More upon*

Analysis of a "Transformation" Tale

Tale	East of the Sun and West of the Moon
Country	Norway
Who changed ?	the prince
Into what ?	white bear
Why ?	his stepmother put a spell on him so he would be a bear by day and a man by night and he had to get someone care for him for a year
What happened ?	the girl goes to live with the bear so her family can be rich finds out that he's really a prince prince has to leave the girl finds him and they get married
Who helps ?	the girl, hags, winds, goodfolk
How did the tale end ?	the prince told the troll to clean his shirt or he would not marry her and the trolls couldn't clean it but the girl could so the prince married her
What things were valued in the tale ?	trust, love, curiosity.

On the back of this paper illustrate the transformation

Figure 8.2   Fifth graders' analysis of transformation tales

a Totem by Christie Harris from Native American lore; and "The Frog Princess" from Russian folk tales.

The group was given 4 days to work on their fairy-tale project. Marlene Fales met with them each day to discuss their reactions to the tales and to give them an opportunity to offer suggestions to each other. Because I was involved in encouraging the project, I received letters from the participants (see Figure 8.3). Their advice included

> ". . . I think other fifth graders would like it also because it's fun and a little easier than other work;"
> "I think it is a very good activity for other fifth and sixth graders but no younger;"
> "I think that doing this really sort of helped you understand the story better so you could enjoy it more."

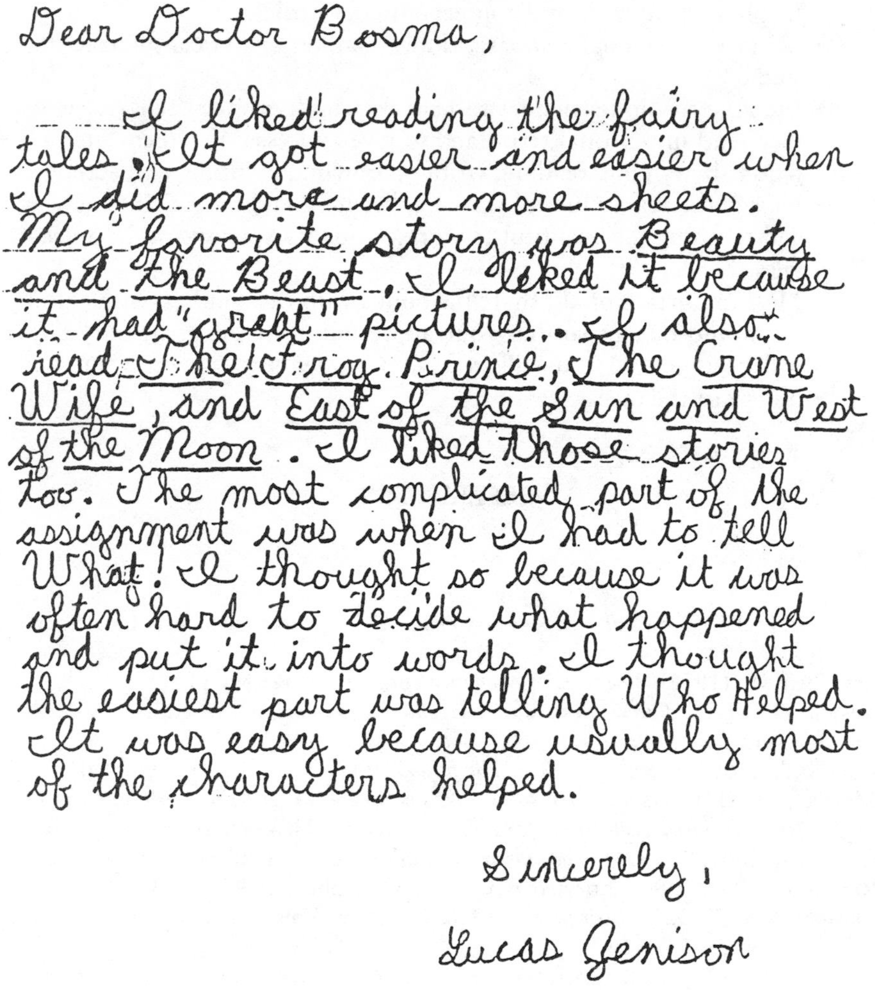

Dear Doctor Bosma,

I liked reading the fairy tales. It got easier and easier when I did more and more sheets. My favorite story was Beauty and the Beast. I liked it because it had "great" pictures. I also read The Frog Prince, The Crane Wife, and East of the Sun and West of the Moon. I liked those stories too. The most complicated part of the assignment was when I had to tell What! I thought so because it was often hard to decide what happened and put it into words. I thought the easiest part was telling Who Helped. It was easy because usually most of the characters helped.

Sincerely,

Lucas Jenison

Figure 8.3 A representative letter from a fifth grader (from Mrs. Fales' room, Sandy Hill, Jenison, Michigan)

SUMMARY

Teachers who introduced fairy tales in the classroom report a high level of enthusiasm among the pupils for reading, listening, writing, viewing art, and investigating the world about them with new vigor. The following guidelines are offered for teachers who wish to develop a study of fairy tales in the classroom:

- Emphasize enjoying and appreciating the stories.
- Nurture a personal response, rather than an analytical or structural study.
- Use analysis and structure to help the children make sense of what they read in personal terms and to give expression to their interpretations by talking, reading, writing, drawing, painting, and acting.
- Engage the reader in oral storying, listening and telling, and viewing and relishing the beautiful artwork of quality versions of the ancient tales.
- Most important of all, share the books with the children with enthusiasm and delight so that your appreciation of the great fairy tales will be inherited and will help your students to see the value and beauty of the tales.

REFERENCES

General

Bauer, C. F. (1977). *Handbook for storytellers*. Chicago: American Library Association.

Bettelheim, B. (1976). *The uses of enchantment*. New York: Knopf.

Bosma, B. (1992). *Fairy tales, fables, legends, and myths* (2nd ed.). New York: Teachers College Press.

Campbell, J., & Moyers, B. (1985). *The power of myth*. New York: Doubleday.

MacDonald, M. R. (1982). *The storyteller's sourcebook: A subject, title and motif index to folklore collections for children*. Detroit: Heal-Schuman.

Opie, I., & Opie, P. (1974). *The classic fairy tale*. London: Oxford University Press.

Ross-Ramon, R. (1980). *Storyteller* (2nd ed.). Columbus, OH: Merrill.

Thompson, S. (1932). *Motif-index of folk literature* (Vols. 1–6). Bloomington: Indiana University Press.

Yolen, J. (1977, Spring). America's Cinderella. *Children's Literature in Education, 8*, 21–29.

Children's Books

Berger, T. (1969). The moss-green princess (pp. 3–14). In *Black fairy tales*. New York: Atheneum.

Bierhorst, J. (1984). *Ring in the prairie*. Illustrated by Leo and Dianne Dillon. New York: Dial.

Cauley, L. B. (1983). *Jack and the beanstalk*. New York: Scholastic.

Chandler, R. (1980). *The frog princess*. Illustrated by Ivan Bilibin. New York: Random House.

Demi. (1980). *Liang and the magic paintbrush.* New York: Holt, Rinehart & Winston.

de Paola, T. (1975). *Strega Nona.* New York: Prentice Hall.

Gag, W. (1982a). *Jorinda and Joringel.* Illustrated by Margot Tomes. New York: Coward, McCann & Geoghegan.

Gag, W. (1982b). *The six swans.* Illustrated by Margot Tomes. New York: Coward, McCann & Geoghegan.

Galdone, P. (1968). *Henny-Penny.* New York: Clarion.

Galdone, P. (1975). *The gingerbread boy.* New York: Seabury.

Grimm, J., & Grimm, W. K. (1972). *Snow-White and the seven dwarfs.* Retold by Randall Jarrell and illustrated by Nancy Burkert. New York: Farrar, Straus & Giroux.

Grimm, J., & Grimm, W. K. (1973). *Tom Thumb.* New York: Atheneum.

Grimm, J., & Grimm, W. K. (1980a). *The fisherman and his wife.* Retold by Randall Jarrell. Illustrated by Margot Zemach. New York: Farrar, Straus & Giroux.

Grimm, J., & Grimm, W. K. (1980b). *Hansel and Gretel.* Retold and illustrated by S. Jeffers. New York: Dial.

Grimm, J., & Grimm, W. K. (1981a). *Cinderella.* Retold and illustrated by Nonny Hogrogian. New York: Greenwillow.

Grimm, J., & Grimm, W. K. (1981b). *The seven ravens.* Retold and illustrated by Lisbeth Zwerger. Saxonville, MA: Picture Book Studio.

Grimm, J., & Grimm, W. K. (1982). *Rapunzel.* Retold by Barbara Rogasky. Illustrated by Trina Schart Hyman. New York: Holiday House.

Grimm, J. & Grimm, W. K. (1984). *The elves and the shoemaker.* Retold and illustrated by Paul Galdone. New York: Clarion.

Hague, K., & Hague, M. (1980). *East of the sun and west of the moon.* New York: Harcourt Brace Jovanovich.

Harris, C. (1973). *Once more upon a totem.* Illustrated by Douglas Tait. New York: Atheneum.

Haviland, V. (1979). Indian Cinderella. In: *North American Legends.* New York: Putnam.

Haviland, V. (1979). Turkey girl. In: *North American Legends* (pp. 94–96). New York: Putnam.

Louie, A. (1982). *Yeh-Shen: A Cinderella story from China.* Illustrated by Ed Young. New York: Philomel.

Littledale, F. (1975). *The elves and the shoemaker.* Illustrated by Brinton Turkle. New York: Four Winds.

Lunn, J. (1979). *The twelve dancing princesses.* Illustrated by Laszlo Gal. New York: Methuen.

Mayer, M. (1978). *Beauty and the beast.* New York: Four Winds.

Morimoto, J. (1984). *Inch boy.* New York: Viking Penguin.

Ransome, A. (1968). *The fool of the world and the flying ship.* Illustrated by Uri Shulevitz. New York: Farrar, Straus & Giroux.

Silverman, M. (1984). *Anna and the seven swans.* New York: Morrow.

Small, E. (1966). *Baba Yaga.* Boston: Houghton Mifflin.

Steele, F. A. (1962). *Tattercoats*. Illustrated by Diane Goode. New York: Macmillan.

Steptoe, J. (1987). *Mufaro's beautiful daughters*. New York: Lothrop, Lee, & Shepard.

Vuong, L. D. (1982). *The brocaded slipper and other Vietnamese tales*. Reading, MA: Addison-Wesley.

Whitney, T. P. (1972). *Vasilisa the beautiful*. New York: Macmillan.

Yabawa, S. (1981). *The crane wife*. Translated by Katherine Paterson. New York: Morrow.

Yolen, J. (1981). *Sleeping ugly*. New York: Coward, McCann & Geoghegan.

Yolen, J. (1986). *The sleeping beauty*. Illustrated by Ruth Sanderson. New York: Knopf.

Zelinsky, P. O. (1986). *Rumpelstiltskin*. New York: Dutton.

Zvorykin, B. (1978). *The firebird*. New York: Viking Penguin.

TRY THIS

Read J. Brett's *The Mitten* (New York: Putnam, 1989), a folktale in picture-book format, to your kindergarten or first-grade class.

1. As follow-up, ask the group to explore the movements of a rabbit, a hedgehog, an owl, a badger, a fox, a bear, and a mouse. Decide with the children how each animal moves by assigning a descriptive verb for each: for instance, a mole creeps; a rabbit hops; a hedgehog scrabbles; an owl struts; a fox slips by; a bear lumbers; a mouse scurries. Place the verbs on the blackboard.
2. Explore the movements of all of the animals with all of the children. In each case encourage all the children to experiment by asking them to try the animal's movement in several ways. For the rabbit, for instance, you might say, "Find two ways to hop like a rabbit." You will be most successful in encouraging creativity if you point out those children who hop (or jump, or otherwise move) differently from the others and if you suggest that there are many ways to move like the animal in question.
3. Assign one animal to each child. If you want to include everyone, several people can be a rabbit, an owl, and so on.
4. Reread the story. While you read, encourage the children to move to the tale. Each animal crawls into the "mitten," a confined area that you define by placing four chairs around the perimeter.
5. When all the animals are in the "mitten," ask them to jump out on signal.

—G.B.

PART III

MAKING CONNECTIONS BETWEEN FOLKLORE AND OTHER FORMS OF LITERATURE

Earlier in this book, we quoted Northrop Frye (1964), who said that we "must know the Bible and the central stories of Greek and Roman" (p. 48) folklore in order to understand modern literature. The chapters in this section are intended as guides for teachers who want to help children take first steps in that direction.

Part III comprises several sections. Dr. Mark Workman, folklorist and English professor, first outlines the approach modern literary critics and folklorists use to analyze literature and folklore. The concepts he explains should help teachers understand why folktales sometimes pop up in modern guise and how teachers themselves can take advantage of the process. Several chapters then introduce teachers to popular trickster folklore, describe similarities to trickster figures in modern literature, and provide guides for teaching. Teachers can use these chapters to become acquainted with important folklore figures, to help them understand similarities between different characters, and to show teachers how to help children understand how authors draw on folklore in modern stories.

Part III can therefore be used in a number of ways: as a vehicle for learning more about literature, as a source for background information and storytelling, and as a guide for teaching connections between folklore and modern literature.

CHAPTER 9

FOLKLORE AND LITERATURE: FROM TEXT TO CONTEXT

Mark Workman

In this pivotal chapter, Mark Workman sketches ways ordinary people create and use folklore. His definition, grounded in up-to-date literary and folklore theory, helps readers see traditional literature as a moveable feast, a treasure that ordinary folk create and pass along to others. Because traditional stories, rhymes, and songs are never quite the same from telling to telling, because folklore of all sorts is constantly moving from person to person and in the process changing, people often come across two versions of the same story, a joke that later turns up as a ghost story, a rhyme that someone uses in a song, a legend that bears an uncanny resemblance to a Bible story.

The process of change so common to folklore is also a key to teaching opportunity. Once teachers understand folklore as an art in flux, once they understand that anyone can change folklore, they can free their pupils to create and vary their own lore, to find it in their own lives and transform stories from one genre to another. Teachers can also use old tales to help children understand the art of literature by known authors. Once they understand that modern authors frequently draw on folktales, elementary school children may come to understand that they, too, are free to draw on old tales, to use them in their own writing, and to find folklore in stories by other people.

Although most of us think of folklore as peripheral to our everyday lives and academic concerns, such perceptions are incorrect. Folklore makes an important, even a profound, difference in our daily lives and in our conceptions of and experiences with literary expressions. Through the jokes and riddles, stories and songs we sing and tell, we define ourselves. The same folklore can also be the wellspring of more formal literature and a vehicle for understanding it.

Folklore commonly connotes sameness, redundancy, routinization. After all, we hear the same jokes and stories over and over again. Over time something that is always the same produces indifference. That which is constant in our lives eventually is transformed into that which is taken for granted and goes unnoticed altogether. A steady, repeated noise soon is taken for granted and ceases to be a noise at all.

Common conceptions of folklore fall into this category. Perhaps once considered lively and enlivening, the selection is typically passed over as residual, a mere leftover or an artifact from a simpler time. With that line of thinking, folkloristics, the study of folklore, becomes little more than a catalogue of curiosities.

EARLY APPROACHES TO FOLKLORE

And that is, in fact, what happened. For a long time, when people studied lore they did little more than create lists and comments. In the eyes of many, folkloristics was a product-oriented discipline, focused not on the dynamics of behavior but on results.

The primary analytical texts, motif and tale-type indexes, which dominated folklore studies into the early 1970s, reflect such an attitude. The indexes, or compendiums of the basic elements and variant forms of tales and similar chronicles, were grounded on the conviction that folkloric texts are fixed, that they travel intact, and that people who reenact the text should strive toward achieving a faithful reproduction. An example can be seen in the clear statement and justification for motif and tale-type indexes seen in Thompson (1946).

The principles reflected in the work of Thompson and others led folklorists to anthologize "canonical" or authorized texts. It also led them to disregard all the complex circumstances of their creation and to overlook all forms of and reasons for local variation. When folklorists went into the field, they focused on salvaging remnants of traditional expression, with little consideration for the manner in which these apparent remnants were produced.

Folklorist Alan Dundes (1969) has characterized this essentially negative attitude as a "devolutionary premise of folkloristics." He meant that, according to this approach, the best, most authentic expression comes first. What follows is merely a broken-down rendition of an "ur" form, a folkloristic term for the oldest form or prototype. The most important task of the folklorist was, therefore, the reconstruction of the primary text. Such an attitude pervades Sir J. G. Frazer's book, *The Golden Bough* (1972).

SIMILARITIES BETWEEN LITERARY CRITICISM AND FOLKLORE: PAST AND PRESENT

It is worth noting that this conception of folklore bears a significant similarity to the New Critical conception of literature, an approach to literary criticism that was highly regarded in the 1940s and 1950s. New Critics considered literature immutable and impermeable. They dismissed as secondary the issues of literary authorship, reception, and the general articulation between literature and the surrounding world. In fact, they regarded the separation between text and context as a defining feature of great art; the students of art tried to eliminate all factors considered peripheral to it. Both folklore and literature were treated as if they were differences that made no difference. Variations were noted, dissected, and anthologized, all with an apparently clinical remoteness and objectivity based on the assumption that one could do things to texts without their doing anything to you.

In today's theoretical environment, this textually oriented approach to cultural expression, whether folklore or literature, seems arid, the attitude underlying this approach untenable. I began by claiming that folklore makes a profound difference in our lives. I am now in a position to explain this claim. The idealized forms delineated by structuralists and the transcendent icons erected by New Critics are insufficient. The picture we once formulated has been subjected to the corrosive (deconstructive) effects of time, transforming once stable constructions into scenes of the ongoing semiotic activity, the signs and symbols of language. Regarded once as enduring in a Platonic manner beyond the moment, folklore is now recognized by contemporary scholars as existing only in performance. Because it is inscribed nowhere else—neither in print, on film, or on vinyl—every rendition of folklore is constrained by the memories of the performer, by the audience, and by the requirements of the current situation. And the memories themselves are always undergoing reconstruction as they are exposed to new experiences and undermined by forgetting. As a result, no two events are ever totally identical in all aspects. At one and the same time, then, folklore is both extremely intimate, because it is produced within relatively small groups in situations where there is face-to-face contact, and it is highly creative in that every performance is an innovative enactment. Each performance is not just re-creative but creative in its own right. (See Toelken, 1979, for an excellent introduction to current thinking on folklore.)

Unlike the literary text that appears to be coterminous with itself, then, the folklore text is not. On the contrary, because folklore is so clearly ephemeral, existing only in unique moments, separating text from the context distorts the folklore. It is the most active locus of memorialization and forgetting. Folklore provides a community with its most immediate and dynamic means of recording and revising its identity. It is not "high" art that defines us as who we are, so much as the often-denigrated folklore, which only the total outcast or lonely survivor is utterly without. So folklore does make a difference. And the difference it makes is profound.

Folklorists are now claiming for literature the same kinds of negotiable, broadly encompassing boundaries that characterize the folk performance. Literature is now regarded as the scene of performance, although in very complex ways. Authors are viewed as the link or nexus for conflicting cultural forces. Readers are not seen as "receiving" meaning passively but as actively "creating" it. (See Foucault, 1989, for a contemporary discussion of authorship.) Texts are viewed not as transcending contexts of origin or reception but as reflections or "mediations" of those sociohistorical moments (Greenblatt, 1989). Whatever metaphors might be used to account for the processes of literary creation or reception, common to all of them is the notion that every aspect of these processes is in some way historically contingent.

When the relationship between folklore and literature was perceived as radically discontinuous, folklorists limited themselves to identifying folkloric motifs and structures embedded within literary texts. As redefined in the ways I have just indicated, however, there is ample cause to look for more significant points of convergence between the two. As it turns out, folklorists have important insights to share with their colleagues in literature departments. There are two important reasons for this: The first has to do with the nature of the subject matter, which so clearly is context-bound; the second has to do with the nature of folklore as a discipline, as much social scientific as humanistic.

Because the discipline calls on social science as well as the humanities, Tristram Coffin (1968) once facetiously described it as "the bastard child of literature and anthropology." It is exactly this bastardization that has proven the strength of the discipline of folklore. Because folkloristics is a composite of sociolinguistics, anthropology, history, and literature, it is well equipped to deal with text conceived of as a cultural event. Although by no means a simple task, it is nevertheless a relatively short move from doing ethnographies of folk performance to doing ethnographies of literary reading.

Because the points of convergence between folklore and literature are actually quite numerous and can be construed in a number of ways, I shall restrict myself to a few specific features of the three loci mentioned above: authors, readers, and texts. Authorship and readership, of course, do not exist in the realm of folklore; the performer and audience take on these functions. Each of these folkloric roles places in the foreground similar but less overt forms of behavior in literature. Like the writer, the folk performer, even when performing singly, is not the exclusive source of her composition; previous enactments echo and reverberate throughout her own perform-ance. As mentioned above, she is also never merely a parrot of the past, even in those situations where exact replication is a cultural ideal. For ex-ample, folklorists have long recognized that some folk cultures place a greater value on innovation than others. The African-American blues tra-dition, for instance, is highly fluid and innovative in its lyrics; the Anglo-American folksong tradition is not. What the folk performer makes explic-itly apparent, therefore, is the truly heteroglossic, many-voiced, quality of all expression, folk or literary.

But even in a conservative folk tradition like the Anglo-American, where performers strive to reproduce a normative text, they cannot. Be-cause folklore is multiply "authored," always performed in face-to-face sit-uations in which the performer and audience directly influence each other, folklore is more overtly "many-voiced" than novels (Bakhtin, 1981). Be-cause they cannot produce a text exactly the same as another produced earlier, folk performers make explicitly apparent the truly heteroglossic quality of their stories. They therefore emphasize the intertextual or inter-woven quality of all expression, folk or literary.

MANY VOICES IN FOLKLORE AND LITERATURE

Two elements contribute to the sense that there are many voices in folklore: the muted presence of tradition, and the much more vocal pres-ence of the audience. As actual witness to the ongoing process of artistic composition, the audience plays a significant role in shaping its form and determining its meaning. The face-to-face contact characteristic of folk per-formance thus places in the foreground the negotiation between the partic-ipants in the event.

As a result, folklorists are not in the least surprised to learn that readers make meanings and that readers belong to interpretative communities (Fish, 1980). They have had a natural laboratory in which to observe and account for the ongoing creation of meaning. Because the folk text highlights the relationship between text and context, they think that environment and cul-ture have significant roles in the discursive structures that give shape to a performance.

They know that even though there is only one version of Coover's (1971) "The Babysitter," there have been and will continue to be literally countless oral reenactments of the tale in folklore. They have found out that each time a folklorist studies a different performance of a folktale with a story similar to "The Babysitter," she is in an excellent position to explain the effects of context on literary canons and on genre formation.

Folklorists are also in a strong position to study context because the canons of folklore are often transformed rapidly as topical factors dictate. Today lore might be concerned with AIDS or the explosion of the *Challenger* space shuttle; tomorrow it might be a concern with race or gender relations, or with ongoing political conflicts and personalities. Similarly, although generic conventions shift more slowly, the folklorist is ideally situated to analyze the rhetorical process of genre formation, inasmuch as the audience may well question the appropriateness and justness of a piece every time a performer tries to satisfy the expectations and affect the convictions of an audience.

CONCLUSIONS: VIEWING LITERATURE FROM THE VIEWPOINT OF FOLKLORISTS

Before proceeding to suggest ways in which folkloristic insights actually apply to reading a specific text, let me review the major contentions of this chapter: First, folklore is a significant, and perhaps, as I have been arguing, even a central, component of human behavior. Second, there exists a greater continuity between oral and written expression than many students of literature have realized heretofore.

The continuity points to a fact that until now has remained largely implicit here, namely, the connection between folkloristics and literary theory: the forms of expression they study. The burden of this essay has been to stress the importance of folkloristics in the study of literature, but the road between the two is bidirectional. The more frequently the passage is traversed in both directions, the more we will come to understand the dynamics of all kinds of expression. As a result, the notion of domains, analytical and cultural, may itself one day be abandoned. One indication that this might be the case is the fact that the canon of literary works appropriate for folklore analysis is considerably expanded by the reconceptualization of folklore-as-process. Thus it is possible to choose texts that at one time would not have received the attention of the folklorist. It is unlikely, for instance, that many folklorists would have considered postmodern literature a proper or fruitful area of folkloristic inquiry. And yet, folklorists can say interesting and significant things even about a mode of literature so apparently antithetical to the spirit of folklore.

For it turns out that postmodernism and folklore are not as unlike as they seem. Perhaps you will recall my claim that folklore provides a community with its most immediate and dynamic means of recording and revising its identity. Phrased differently, folk expression marks the sight not just of tradition but of emergence (Williams, 1977), as well. The link between folklore and postmodernism is especially apparent in performance; for it is then that innovation in folklore occurs, and it is in performance that the realization of the suggestive postmodern text occurs. In folk performance traditions are stretched to include the needs of the moment; in postmodern performance, the cultural resources of the reader are marshalled to forge a newly meaningful, which is to say a socially revitalized, language.

Consider, for instance, the experience of reading Thomas Pynchon's *Gravity's Rainbow* (1973), a book that many critics call the *Moby Dick* of 20th-century American literature. The novel chronicles the adventures of the hero, Tyrone Slothrop, who last appears in the novel as "an intersection of possibilities" about 150 pages prior to its conclusion, during and immediately after World War II. Conspiring against Slothrop, a kind of 20th-century Huck Finn, are the forces of War and Empire, which, according to the narrator, "expedite barriers between our lives." Although War actually divides and subdivides people through its propaganda, it always appears to stress unity, alliance, pulling together; but it does not appear to want a folk consciousness, not even the sort the Germans engineered under Hitler: "ein Volk, ein Führer." It wants a machine of many separate parts and it wants complexity, not oneness. But whereas War and Empire appear to suppress folk consciousness, Pynchon himself is very much in favor of it.

Folklore, therefore, enters into Pynchon's novel in a number of conventional and unconventional ways, from accurate descriptions of oral-formulaic composition of Asiatic nomads to "proverbs for paranoids" of his own devising.

Important as the folkloric content of the novel is, however, the dynamic that exists between the novel and the reader is also important. Here a warlike approach to canonical criticism (that is, criticism that leads us to approach the text as a fixed, aesthetic artifact) will serve to erect barriers between reader and a highly resistant text. Pynchon therefore promotes a new attitude toward reading his novel. The reader, like the hero, becomes an intersection of possibilities, one who possesses a folk consciousness. It is folk consciousness that is characterized by openness to what Pynchon calls "the risks of the moment," those precious occasions when we see things anew and fashion a more vital, more intimate language, a folk language for representing them (Workman, 1983).

With a novel like *Gravity's Rainbow*, therefore, the process of reading comes to resemble a kind of folkloric activity; author and reader, both broadly conceived, converge in the text and, recognizing the historically contingent nature of all expression and all interpretation, together produce an emergent or creolized response. It is in such readings that the ethnographic talents of the folklorist may be brought to bear.

Similarly, the same kinds of connections can be made between folklore and children's literature. Fifth graders reading a book like *Maniac Magee* (Spinelli, 1990), for instance, can easily see the connection between Maniac himself and Cinderella. They can also be encouraged to draw upon their own folk consciousness in their reading. As a result, teachers can help their pupils understand more about the stories themselves, about the culture in which they were written, and about the interconnections within literature. Their comprehension will deepen, their pleasure in reading increase.

REFERENCES

Bakhtin, M. (1981). *The dialogic imagination.* Translated by M. Holquist and C. Emerson. Austin: University of Texas Press.

Coffin, T. (1968). *Our living traditions: An introduction to American folklore.* New York: Basic Books.

Coover, R. (1971). The babysitter. In S. S. Elkins, *Stories from the sixties.* New York: Doubleday.

Dundes, A. (1969). The devolutionary premise of folklore theory. *Journal of the Folklore Institute, 6,* 5–19.

Foucault, M. (1989). What is an author? In R. C. Davis and R. Schiefer (Eds.), *Contemporary literary criticism* (2nd ed.) London: Longmans.

Fish, S. (1980). *Is there a text in this class?* Cambridge, MA: Harvard University Press.

Frazer, J. G. (1972). *The golden bough.* New York: Macmillan.

Greenblatt, S. (1989). Toward a poetics of culture. In H. A. Veeser, *The new historicism.* London: Routledge Kegan Paul.

Pynchon, T. (1973). *Gravity's rainbow.* New York: Viking.

Thompson, S. (1946). *The folktales.* New York: Holt.

Toelken, B. (1979). *The dynamics of folklore.* Boston: Houghton Mifflin.

Williams, R. (1977). *Marxism and literature.* New York: Oxford University Press.

Workman, M. (1989, Spring). Folklore in the wilderness: folklore and postmodernism. *Midwestern Folklore, 15.*

TRY THIS

1. Introduce your class to one or more urban legends, for instance, "The Babysitter" (Brunvand, 1981), telling the children that the story is "true," that you got it from a friend of a friend.
2. Then tell the group how urban legends start and how they are passed along. Introduce the class to more urban legends by having available the following books:

    Brunvand, J. H. (1984). *The choking doberman and other "new" urban legends.* New York: Norton.
    Brunvand, J. H. (1986). *The Mexican pet: More new urban legends and some old favorites.* New York: Norton.
    Brunvand, J. H. (1981). *The vanishing hitchhiker: American urban legends and their meanings.* New York: Norton.

   Encourage the boys and girls to retell the stories they have heard or read.
3. Introduce the children to short stories, movies, or novels, that in some way use urban legends in their stories. Some examples are *Are You in the House Alone?* (World Vision Home Video), which is taken from the novel of the same name by Richard Peck (1976) or *Adventures in Babysitting* (Touchstone Video). Show the class one or both of the videotapes and then help them locate the urban legends referred to in the movie. Ask the boys and girls how and why they think the writer used the urban story in the movie. Did they retell the story, changing it to suit their own purposes or did they simply refer to the story? (*Are You in the House Alone?* simply retells a variant of the story. *Adventures in Babysitting* contains a number of sight jokes that refer to a variety of urban legends.)

—G.B.

CHAPTER 10

❀ NANABOZHOO: SUPERMAN OF THE GREAT LAKES INDIANS

Alethea K. Helbig

In this interesting chapter Alethea Helbig, English professor, expert on children's literature, and author of *Nanabozhoo, Giver of Life* (1987), tells Nanabozhoo stories that emphasize the range of his personality. Among other stories, she recounts how he brought fire and other boons to the Indians; how he destroyed Pearl Feather, a terrible monster who lived on the other side of Lake Michigan; and how he brought hot summer weather to Michigan. Although Professor Helbig tells a number of tales that made Nanabozhoo a special favorite of the Great Lakes Indians, she also makes it clear that in many ways he was completely interchangeable with other well-known tricksters such as Coyote, Raven, and Anansi.

Teachers will find the stories about Nanabozhoo useful in class. Because some of the tales are suited to storytelling sessions, the teachers can learn the stories in the chapter that follows and retell them in their classes. They can also use Nanabozhoo in their classes as a focus for discussion. The children will enjoy comparing him with other tricksters like Anansi, or Hershel of Ostropol, or with tricksters from modern literature. In the process the children may gain insight into character development in folklore and modern literature.

The North Central Indians told many stories about a hero who might be called the all-purpose hero/buffoon of his people. A terrible rascal and a beneficent creator, Nanabozhoo is the main figure of oral tradition of the North Central Woodland Indians who occupy the forested area from the Ohio River to Hudson Bay, and from the Albany River in New York State to the Mississippi. In this vast region lived many tribes belonging to the same language family. Collectively called Algonkians by scholars, they were known among themselves as Anishinabeg. Among these are the Ojibwa (Chippewa), Ottawa, and Potawatomi.

NANABOZHOO: A COMPLEX FIGURE

The folklore heritage of these Indians has revolved around a mythological figure who is known by a variety of names: Nenebuc, Nanabush, Menaboju, Wenebush, Winabojo, and Nanabozhoo. Whatever form the name takes, it has usually meant something like "foolish fellow" or "great rabbit." Because Nanabozhoo sometimes appears as a little woodlands rabbit, both meanings are appropriate for describing his deeds, which are both foolish and great.

How can this figure be a hero and a buffoon at the same time? Very simply because he is a complex creation. As a trickster, Nanabozhoo is a curiously elusive and many-sided character, both evil and good, rogue and benefactor, destroyer and creator, a simpleton and a culture hero. As superhero or Indian extraordinary, Nanabozhoo provides the stimulus for many entertaining legends told in the lodges on long winter nights. His adventures are still on the lips of many people today. So numerous are the stories about him that it has been a common saying that no one person could tell them all.

Although details vary from place to place and teller to teller, and there are many fascinating variations, the stories about Nanabozhoo are consistent enough to be summarized in this way.

He is of miraculous birth, the son of a virgin and the West Wind. Raised by his maternal grandmother, he wages warfare with monsters and performs heroic and marvelous deeds, experiencing a catastrophe like that of Jonah and a deluge like Noah's. He is responsible for such cultural necessities as the canoe, corn, and the arts of healing, as well as numerous natural phenomena, but he also wanders the earth playing tricks and being tricked. In later life he develops into a wise man and prophet whose advice and boons are sought.

We can appreciate the Nanabozhoo stories on a number of levels. At the simplest one, the stories are full of amusement and adventure. At a somewhat higher level, they are didactic, conveying information and morals about virtues and vices and their respective consequences for both children and adults. Because he is a rogue and buffoon who usually pays for his tricks and foolishness, Nanabozhoo illustrates how people should not behave. On a still higher plane of significance, the Indians saw themselves reflected in the trickster's life and adventures. They identified with Nanabozhoo's good qualities and successes and derived vicarious satisfaction from the way he flouted established mores and later got his comeuppances. Behind all the tomfoolery, didactic lessons, the identification and satisfaction, the Anishinabeg saw him, and still see him, essentially as a life-giver.

NANABOZHOO: THE GREEDY

Nanabozhoo is often a ridiculous figure; the situations in which he finds himself are frequently absurd. His lack of common sense and inability to look ahead provide the occasion for many rollicking good legends like the following story in which he is punished for his greed and thoughtlessness in a poetically just way:

One day as he is walking along, Nanabozhoo encounters a buffalo cow, which he slays for food for himself and his family. As he is butchering the cow, a hungry porcupine comes by and asks for a share of the meat, but Nanabozhoo refuses him. He gives the porcupine a good hard kick, which sends the starving creature scampering away.

After he hides the meat under some bushes, Nanabozhoo rushes to his lodge to get his family to help him carry the meat home, but while he is gone, the porcupine comes back and steals the meat, carrying it up into a high pine tree that overhangs a river. When Nanabozhoo returns, he finds his cache of meat gone. He and his family scour the area until he discovers what he thinks is his meat under the water near the bank of the river, with the porcupine sitting nearby, underwater too, guarding it.

Nanabozhoo dives repeatedly to recover his meat, failing each time, of course. Finally, he ties a large stone to his feet to weigh himself down so he can remain underwater long enough to pry loose the supposed cache. To his consternation, he finds he can't rise back to the surface. With tremendous effort, his lungs almost bursting from lack of air, he manages to untie the rock, but not before he has swallowed so much water he is bloated to the size of a bear.

While resting on the bank, he happens to glance upward and is surprised to see his meat in the tree overhead, the porcupine on the branch beside it. He realizes he has almost killed himself diving for a reflection.

NANABOZHOO: A COLOSSAL BLUNDERER

Nanabozhoo often appears as a colossal blunderer who does not think before he acts.

> Once as he is traveling with his grandmother, carrying the old lady on his back, they happen to pass a grove of oak trees where there are lots of acorns on the ground. The old woman suggests that he stop and put her down on a stump nearby so that they can gather the nuts. Taking her instructions quite literally, he stops immediately and tosses the old lady toward the stump, knocking her unconscious. He begins then to gather the acorns, grumbling all the while about how unfair his grandmother is to leave him to do the work. When the old lady comes to, she cries, "Oh, Nanabozhoo! Whenever I ask you to do something, you always go to extremes!"

This story, like many others about Nanabozhoo, is probably a satire on human behavior, on how people don't use their heads.

Since the Anishinabeg believed that it is a virtue to be yourself, the "borrowed plumes" theme occurs in a number of variant forms. Nanabozhoo attempts to fly with the birds—flying looks like such fun!—but he plummets to the ground, knocking the wind out of himself in landing. In another story he admires the beaver's tail, which makes an interesting "plinking" sound on the ice in the winter. So he asks the beaver to pin a tail of some sort on him. But no matter how hard Nanabozhoo tries, he can't make his tail go "plink! plink!" like the beaver's.

Nanabozhoo seldom remembers instructions. Once, when he encounters a snipe jumping from log to log in Lake Superior, Nanabozhoo wishes to do the same thing. It looks so exciting. The snipe tells him to follow close behind him, saying as he jumps, "Big Sea Water with a hole in it." He tells Nanabozhoo especially not to say "Sea closes." But since Nanabozhoo has no staying power, he soon tires of saying the same thing all the time. So he says "Sea closes," just for variety. Then down he plunges between two logs, out of sight in the icy lake water.

On the whole, Nanabozhoo lacks common sense and foresight. He overeats until he can only lie and wait for his stomach to go down, unable to move or even to defend himself. Attracted once by a particularly delicious-looking root plant, he gorges on it, only to discover, to his dismay, that it has powerful and quick-acting laxative properties.

He is annoyed by the sound of the wind singing through a hollow pine tree. The wind goes in one big knothole and out another. So Nanabozhoo sticks his arm through the holes as hard as he can, blocking the wind and stopping the sound, only to discover that he can't get his arm back out. He is stuck and has to stay there all night long, cold and hungry, until a big storm comes up and blows the tree down.

Highly inquisitive, he seldom can control his curiosity. He wonders what it is like inside a dried-out buffalo skull, so he changes himself into an ant and crawls inside. Then he forgets himself in his pleasure at rummaging around in there and changes back into his human form. His head gets stuck inside the skull, and, unable to see where he is going, he bumps into animals and bangs into trees. He is released when he accidentally stumbles over a stone, falls down, and cracks the skull open against the stone.

Nanabozhoo hears some spooky noises once while walking home from fishing, but it is such a dark night that he cannot see very well. He loses control completely, drops the fish he has caught, and races back to his lodge, where his grandmother informs him that the spooky noises had been made by owls out to get his fish. They had counted on him to panic, and Nanabozhoo, true to form not thinking, lost his head and overreacted.

On the whole, Nanabozhoo's comic adventures not only are interesting and amusing, but also illustrate vividly what will happen if one does not practice certain virtues. The tales caution against being boastful, wasteful, and so naive that one is easily tricked or taken advantage of. But to cooperate with one's fellows, to use one's common sense, to live with moderation, to look ahead and consider possible courses of action—these are lessons implicitly conveyed by the tales of Nanabozhoo. These are virtues the Anishinabeg valued and traits they wanted future generations to cherish and practice.

NANABOZHOO: A RELIGIOUS FIGURE

Although the legends about Nanabozhoo are intended both to entertain and to teach moral values, Nanabozhoo is primarily a religious figure at the very heart of Woodlands mythology. He is a rogue and buffoon, but also a leader and demigod who creates and regulates the world.

Growing up under the care of his grandmother, Nanabozhoo early develops great size, strength, wisdom, and courage. Because of these qualities he achieves worthy ends for which he is later remembered and admired. Because at first he is in the form of a little rabbit, his grandmother calls him Nanabozhoo, meaning "great rabbit." She thereby predicts that he will do great deeds.

One day he sits up on his haunches and hops slowly across the floor of the lodge, the whole earth trembling each time his body touches the ground.

The evil spirits who dwell underground become uneasy because they recognize that a great and powerful spirit, who is good and will wage war against them, has been born. Already when Nanabozhoo is very young, two separate and conflicting sets of beings become aware of his future greatness: his grandmother, who is good, and the spirits below, who are evil. Later on, in his youth, Nanabozhoo's father, the West Wind, informs him that it is his destiny to use his great strength and keen wit for the good of people by making the earth safe for them and by providing them with the means for easier, better lives. The West Wind promises his son that after Nanabozhoo's work on earth is finished, there will be a place for him in the North with his elder brother, the North Wind, as a mighty wind spirit. So it is that in his youth Nanabozhoo learns from his father that a divine plan governs his life.

Obeying his father's command, Nanabozhoo soon undertakes a series of tasks to improve the world. He embarks upon the dangerous exploit of destroying a terrible monster, Pearl Feather, who lives on the other side of Lake Michigan or Lake Superior from his grandmother's lodge. [Accounts vary.] This monster is terrorizing the area around the lake and is causing trouble for the people who live there.

Hearing that Nanabozhoo is coming, Pearl Feather orders the great fish who lives in the lake to swallow Nanabozhoo. When the great fish obligingly does so, Nanabozhoo coolly looks around to see what it is like in there and how he might escape. He discovers in the darkness about him his friends Bear, Porcupine, Buffalo, Elk, Raven, Squirrel, and others. Those who have been inside the fish for a long time are in a bad way. This makes Nanabozhoo so angry that he seizes his war club and strikes the great fish a savage blow to the heart, causing the fish to become nauseated.

For a while Nanabozhoo is afraid that the fish might disgorge him into the middle of the lake, but with the help of Squirrel, he manages to shove his canoe across the fish's throat, blocking the passage out. Because Squirrel has willingly helped him, Nanabozhoo gives him his name. Thereafter, Squirrel is called Adjidaumo, which means "bottoms up," an appropriate name for a squirrel. Nanabozhoo continues his attack on the fish's heart and finally succeeds in killing the creature.

The body of the fish drifts to shore, coming to rest on the bank, where seagulls help Nanabozhoo and his friends to get out by scratching an opening in the side of the fish with their claws. To reward the seagulls for their assistance, Nanabozhoo bestows upon all seagulls beauty of body and grace in flight. Then he chops up the great fish and casts the pieces into the lake, creating the first small lake fishes.

The subsequent battle against the monstrous Pearl Feather is hard and long. When Nanabozhoo has only three arrows left and is beginning to get worried, a woodpecker whispers in his ear that Pearl Feather has one vulnerable spot, on the crown of his head under a certain lock of hair. Following the bird's advice, Nanabozhoo aims at the indicated place and kills the monster, ridding the people of the lake of their tormentor. Then he takes a little of Pearl Feather's blood and touches it to the woodpecker's head. To this day, some woodpeckers have red heads in memory of their ancestor who helped Nanabozhoo slay the monster of the lake.

Besides killing monsters and evil spirits during his lifetime, Nanabozhoo also fulfills his culture-hero role by recreating the world after the flood. This is the most popular and widespread story about him.

Many evil water spirits rise up from their watery home to get revenge on him for killing their prince. Bringing their waters with them, they flood the whole earth as they chase Nanabozhoo, who flees for sanctuary to the top of a mountain. There he observes some small animals struggling in the water, looking for a place to rest. He asks each of them to dive down and bring up dirt so he can make a new earth. The loon, the otter, and the beaver all try but are drowned in the attempt. Finally, when it is the muskrat's turn, he, too, loses his life, but his body rises to the surface, and under his claws Nanabozhoo discovers a little mud. Using his divine power, he rolls the dirt around in his hand and shapes it into a ball, which he increases in size until it eventually becomes a small island from which the new earth is formed. Then Nanabozhoo brings the drowned animals back to life and rewards them for their efforts to help him by providing them with an appropriate habitat and food. Thus Nanabozhoo becomes a creator after evil spirits have destroyed the earth.

When he acquires fire, Nanabozhoo not only jeopardizes his life but endures pain and suffering.

One morning when Nanabozhoo wakes up, it is bitter cold in the lodge he shares with his grandmother. When he remarks to her that he wishes that they had some fire with which to warm themselves, she replies that that is impossible because only the sun, who lives very far away across the lake in a lodge guarded by powerful spirits, has fire. Nanabozhoo, who is young and strong, ambitious and energetic, soon comes up with the idea of building a canoe fashioned cleverly of birch bark, the first of its kind ever made. He instructs his grandmother to prepare a pot with dry tinder that will burn easily. She must be sure to have it ready for him when he returns.

He paddles across the lake, soon arriving at the sun's lodge where he changes into the form of a rabbit. He lies on the shore of the lake, pretending to be half-drowned from the waves. The two pretty daughters of the sun find him, take pity on him, carry him home to their lodge, and place him by the fire to dry out.

As soon as he recovers, he hops and scampers friskily about the lodge in such an amusing fashion that even the sun is entertained by his antics. When a big smile spreads over the sun's face, sparks from the sun's smile land on Nanabozhoo's back, igniting some tinder that he had fastened between his shoulders. As soon as he feels the heat through his fur, Nanabozhoo hops as fast as he can back to his canoe and, with the help of the wind spirits, speeds homeward. His grandmother races toward him with the firepot as soon as she sees him coming and quickly shakes off enough fire to start a blaze in the pot. Nanabozhoo hurts in many places and is quite miserable because the fire has burned through his fur coat, but in a few days, he is as lively as ever after his grandmother puts herbs on his burns.

NANABOZHOO: A REGULATOR AND TRANSFORMER

In the new world after the flood, Nanabozhoo acts as a regulator and transformer, bringing about many features of the landscape, as well as animal and vegetable life. Henry Rowe Schoolcraft (Williams, 1956), an early 19th-century collector of Algonkian tales and a chronicler of the life of this hero, says that there is hardly a promontory or unusually shaped hill or rock formation that is not in some way connected with Nanabozhoo.

One story tells about a trip Nanabozhoo takes to the Straits of Mackinac. He can't figure out how to get across to the Lower Peninsula, but after pondering his problem for a while, he builds a bridge with rocks taken from the shore of Lake Michigan, thereby bringing the first Big Mack bridge into being. After he crosses the lake, a storm comes up, destroying his bridge and leaving the remains of that first bridge in Mackinac, Round, and Bois Blanc Islands.

In a late story, which shows White influence, Nanabozhoo comes out the winner in an argument with Paul Bunyan about logging pine trees. And that is why there are large pine forests standing in the Great Lakes region yet today.

Nanabozhoo is also responsible for the peculiar identifying features and the behavior and habitat of many animals. He causes ducks to have flat backs and gives some of them red eyes. He gives the snowshoe rabbits flat, yellowish feet and woodchucks gray coats. Because he once tosses a turtle into a pond many turtles have liked to live in or near water ever since. He punishes the raccoon for its insensitivity to the crayfish by condemning it to a life in the trees and causes humps to grow on the backs of buffalo because they so carelessly trample small animals when they gallop over the countryside. He sentences foxes to dens underground because they are the allies of the buffalo. He gives roses thorns for protection against rabbits, which have overgrazed on roses, bringing them to the point of extinction.

Moreover, Nanabozhoo fixes the seasons and creates the weather. Anybody who has ever lived in the Great Lakes region knows that the weather is very changeable, fair and pleasant one day, dark and disagreeable the next. The Anishinabeg associated this phenomenon with Nanabozhoo, too, some saying that if it had not been for Nanabozhoo it would always be dark, gloomy, and cold in these regions.

> Nanabozhoo has a friend, Pee-puck-e-wis, with whom he runs a race, starting in the south somewhere. As long as Nanabozhoo is in the lead, the weather is pleasant and sunny, with flowers growing, birds singing, and animals gamboling happily in the woods. But Pee-puck-e-wis grows jealous of his friend's progress and of the pleasantness of the journey. He scoops up water and throws it into the air, causing rain. He calls upon the East Wind to push dark clouds over the sky, and asks the West Wind to blow cold and icy air across Nanabozhoo's path. But whenever Nanabozhoo looks back and smiles, the clouds pass away, the icy blasts die down, and the sun shines again. In this way, Nanabozhoo brings warm spring and hot summer weather to Michigan.
>
> Because of Pee-puck-e-wis, the summer is not consistently warm, and the weather changes frequently. After Nanabozhoo passes around Lake Superior and heads back south, Pee-puck-e-wis is free to cause the weather to become cold once more. The next year the two resume their race, and the same thing happens again. It still happens today. Whenever the weather changes rapidly and sharply, according to the stories, Nanabozhoo and Pee-puck-e-wis are close by, running their race again.

In his benefactor role, Nanabozhoo gives the Indians many good and useful gifts. He invents the canoe, lances, hatchets, and arrow points, and gives them to the people for their use. He names the plants so that people can identify them and teaches them their uses. He steals tobacco from a troublesome giant and gives it to people for their ceremonies. At some point in his career, in a wrestling match he defeats a tall youth dressed in green, named Mandomin. Mandomin then gives Nanabozhoo directions for preparing the earth in a certain way and commands that Nanabozhoo bury his body in the soil. The plant that springs from Mandomin's buried body is corn.

Nanabozhoo teaches his people how to use herbs for healing and institutes the special religious rites and chants of the Medicine Lodge. So that the earth might not become overpopulated, Nanabozhoo decrees that people shall die and puts one of his brothers in charge of the place of the dead. And the stories go on and on, presenting Nanabozhoo as the kind helper and teacher of his people and as a powerful changer and regulator in nature.

The stories don't say how long Nanabozhoo lives on earth. He marries and has a family, and as he grows older, gradually loses his reputation as culture hero-trickster-buffoon, becoming more of a magician and wise man. He moves somewhere to the East, according to the Menomini; or to an ice floe far to the North in Canada, according to the Potawatomi; or far to the West, according to some Ojibwa. Others say he becomes a sleeping giant rock formation that can be seen in Thunder Bay just off the western shore of Lake Superior. But there are also stories connecting him with Mackinac Island where, as an aged man, he is said to live in a lodge with a pointed roof.

Wherever he makes his home, there are legends of people journeying to make requests of him. The humblest and least selfish requests please him most. In his wisdom he specially rewards those people he considers most worthy but punishes arrogant and selfish petitions. Once 10 young men travel to his lodge on Mackinac Island. One by one he hears and grants their requests, but with increasing impatience as their appeals become more and more presumptuous and selfish. Finally, when one of the men asks for everlasting life, Nanabozhoo grows very angry.

He tells the youth he will give him what he asks for. He tells him that henceforth he will stand as a monument to the arrogance and pride of youth. Then, before the horrified eyes of his friends, the young man's body enlarges, becomes twisted and contorted, until finally it hardens into a tall rock formation. Some say this rock formation is the one known today as Sugar Loaf Rock, a prominent tourist attraction on Mackinac Island.

Another tale says that after he has completed his work on earth, Nanabozhoo is taken by his father, the West Wind, to the far North to assume the position he has been promised among the winds. Thereafter, he rules over the Northwest, sharing that quarter with an older brother. Other stories say, however, that he can sometimes still be seen near Mackinac, where he had his lodge. There he appears as a little white rabbit skittering about in the snow, looking things over and checking up on the world. Nanabozhoo, the stories go, who did many good things to help his people, sometimes at great cost to himself, is still concerned for the welfare of his people and still watching over them. Whether trickster, fool, or benefactor, Nanabozhoo remains the lifegiver of the Anishinabeg.

REFERENCE

Williams, M. (Ed.). (1956). *Schoolcraft's Indian legends*. East Lansing: Michigan State University Press.

TRY THIS

Tell a group of children several Nanabozhoo stories. Then ask them to decide how he behaves in each story. Is he a fool, a hero, a life-giver, a moral leader? The following matrix will help boys and girls understand how Nanabozhoo varies from story to story:

Comparison chart for Nanabozhoo stories

Story	Fool	Hero	Lifegiver	Moral leader	Trickster
#1					
#2					
#3					

Ask the group why the Indians may have given Nanabozhoo so many different qualities.

Next ask the children to act out one or more of the following picture books by P. Goble (all published by Orchard Books, New York, NY) using a reader's theater approach:

Iktomi and the Ducks (1990)
Iktomi and the Buffalo Skull (1991)
Iktomi and the Berries (1989)
Iktomi and the Boulder (1991)

(One individual should read the part printed in large black print, another reads the gray print, a third reads the small black print. Another child should sing the song in *Iktomi and the Buffalo Skull*.) When the children have read a story aloud, ask how the two tricksters (Iktomi and Nanabozhoo) are alike and different from each other. (They are, in most respects, exactly the same; but Nanabozhoo also brings good things to mankind.) Finally, ask the group if real people can be both good and bad.

—G.B.

CHAPTER 11

❈ ANANSI, A HERO FOR ALL SEASONS

Naomi Barnett and Gloria T. Blatt

In this chapter by Barnett and Blatt, readers meet Anansi, the African-American trickster. In some ways he is exactly like Nana-bozhoo and Iktomi; in other ways he is a unique figure who changed as the Africans moved from Africa to the Caribbean and North and South America.

The changes help readers in a variety of ways. First, they open a window on the history of African-Americans. Second, through them we gain some insight into the folklore process, and trickster figures in particular. Third, they offer teachers rich opportunities for instruction.

Anansi, the trickster of the American South, the Caribbean, and Africa, is a popular hero of numerous tales. His character and the stories about him first appeared in West Africa among the Ashanti and their neighbors. The tales they told and those that others told later continue to be favorites among their descendants in the Caribbean, North and South Carolina, and parts of Central America. The stories themselves, as well as the names they used for Anansi, reflect important shifts in their own lives and are thus fertile ground for comparison.

Although individual tribes and slaves used different names (Clarkson & Cross, 1980) for him (e.g., Gizo among the Hausas, Kwaku Ananse among the Ashanti), the complex character of the trickster hero was essentially the same throughout West Africa. He was the spider god from whom all humanity was descended. At times soft and gentle, he could also be artful and secretive. He tried to fool others, but he often was fooled himself. Wily and foolish, subtle and outrageous at the same time, he was the accomplice of man and the rival of the high gods. All in all, he was a lovable, cunning rogue, a prince of a fellow.

In the New World he also had a variety of names (Clarkson & Cross, 1980): Mr. or Bro Nancy, Bro Anancy, and Spiderman Anansy or Anancy in various parts of the Caribbean, Miss Nancy in South Carolina, and Aunt Nancy in the Gullah region. In all of these places he took on a variety of shapes. Sometimes he was a man, sometimes a spider, sometimes a man with spidery appendages. He still played tricks on others and could be soft and gentle, scheming and secretive. He still was a fool caught by his own tricks, still wily and stupid, outrageous and subtle at the same time. But on occasion he could also be a hero. All in all, he remained a prince of a fellow.

Even though there were striking similarities between Kwaku Ananse, the Ashanti hero, and Bro Nancy, et al., the New World trickster hero, there were also major differences between the two. In the Old World, Ananse directed his tricks toward the high gods; in the New World, Bro Anancy tried to trick powerful neighbors like Tiger. His cunning and scheming reflected the indirection and occasionally the victory that the black man experienced in a racist society (Brathwaite, 1971; Dance, 1985).

SOME AFRICAN STORIES ABOUT KWAKU ANANSE

Because Kwaku Ananse was placed in the pantheon of Ashanti gods, tales from West Africa reveal something of the religious beliefs of the storytellers. In one story Ananse creates the earth. In another he brings fire to the people and to Nzambi-Mangu in heaven. In still another, a favorite in Africa and the New World alike, he decides to gain power over all the Ananse stories.

HOW KWAKU ANANSE GOT THE ANANSE STORIES

When Ananse makes his way to the heavens and asks for the stories, Nyame agrees to give them to him but also asks him to pay a price. First Kwaku Ananse must bring Nyame three things: a swarm of *mmoboro,* or living hornets; Onini the python, and Osebo the leopard.

Ananse cuts a gourd from a vine and makes a small hole in it. Then he goes into the bush where the hornets live, singing, "The rain is coming, the rain is coming." The hornets doubt that it is coming because they see nothing, so Kwaku Ananse says, "Soon, soon. If the water gets on you, you can get into this gourd and stay dry."

He leaves the hornets and pours water over himself so that he is dripping wet. Then he tells the hornets, "See, the rain is falling. It is following me. Enter the gourd quick, quick."

When the hornets enter the gourd, Ananse plugs the hole with grass and carries the gourd to Nyame. The god of Heaven accepts them and says, "Yes, you have paid part of the price, but there is more to pay."

So Kwaku Ananse returns to the woods. He cuts a long bamboo pole and goes to Onini the python, talking to himself and saying, "My wife is wrong; I am right. My wife says he is shorter; I say he is longer. My wife demeans him; I respect him."

Onini the python overhears him and asks, "Why do you quarrel with your wife?"

"We argue about you. I say you are long, long. My wife says you are short, short. I say you are longer than this pole. My wife says you are shorter than this pole."

So Ananse lays the pole on the ground and the python lies beside it.

"You seem a little short," he says. So Onini stretches himself out.

"A little more," Anansi says. "You are still a little short." The python tries again.

"No," he says. "I cannot stretch any further."

"When you stretch out at one end, you get shorter at the other," suggests Ananse. "I will tie you in the front so that you don't slip back."

He ties Onini first at his head, then in the middle, and finally at the other end. The python cannot move.

"My wife was right," says Ananse. "I was wrong. You are shorter than the pole." Ananse picks up the pole with the python lashed to it and takes him to Nyame. Once again Nyame says, "You have paid more of the price, but your next task is hard, hard." Ananse goes into the woods where he digs a pit because Osebo, the leopard, often comes there in the dark of the night. Ananse covers the hole with thick branches and scatters leaves and dust on top. Then he waits a short way from the pit. When Osebo comes in the dark, dark night, he cannot see the pit. He falls in.

The next morning when Ananse comes by, Osebo calls up to him, "Help me get out of here."

"Yes," answers Kwaku Ananse, "but if I help you, you will one day eat me."

"I promise I will not," Osebo promises.

So Ananse bends a sapling over the pit, ties it down, and then ties another cord to the sapling and throws it down to Osebo saying, "Tie the cord to your tail." Osebo does as he was told.

When he is sure that the tail is well tied, Ananse cuts the vine with his knife. For a moment, he holds the sapling down with his foot. When he lets go, the tree springs up, jerking the leopard out of the pit. Back and forth, back and forth Osebo swings, twisting in the air. When Ananse has killed him, he carries the body to the house of Nyame.

"This is the third price."

"Because you have paid all the prices, from this time forward, all stories about Ananse will belong to you, Kwaku Ananse." (A variant of this story appears in Courlander, 1947, p. 586.)

It is interesting to note that when the same story is told in the Caribbean, Ananse usually pays the price to Tiger, a powerful neighbor, not Nyame (Berry, 1988).

In another story Ananse steals a magic hoe. Because he does not completely understand the magic involved, he accidentally gives the hoe to all the world.

HOW KWAKU ANANSE STOLE THE HOE

Kwaku Ananse and Kotoko, the porcupine, join together to begin a farm. First, it is Ananse's turn to work in the field. He takes his family and works all day with his bush knife.

Then it is Kotoko's turn. He comes to the field with a magic hoe; he raises it and sings,

> Give me a hand,
> Give me a hand,
> Oh, hoe of Kotoko.

Magically, the hoe begins to work all by itself while Kotoko rests in the shade of a tree. It cuts up the earth and turns it over until all is clear. When the night comes, the porcupine says other words and the hoe stops all by itself.

Ananse sees how the hoe works and wants it for himself. He goes that very night and steals it from the porcupine. Then early the next morning he brings it to the farm saying the magic words:

> Give me a hand,
> Give me a hand,
> Oh, hoe of Kotoko.

The hoe begins to work. It cultivates the earth while Ananse sits in the shade resting. But he does not pay any attention to it. It moves across the field, into the dense bush everywhere clearing the ground. Then, because Ananse does not know the word to stop it, it hoes its way to the edge of the land and across the sea to the land of the

White People. There the people fashion many hoes just like it and bring it to the Ashanti. (A version of this story appears in Courlander, 1947, p. 596.)

Even in the early stories from Africa, Ananse is multifaceted. He brings boons to mankind, but he also is greedy and impulsive. In one story he collects the wisdom in the world but impulsively throws it away. As is often the case, it is greed that gets him into trouble.

ANANSE AND THE POT OF WISDOM

Kwaku Ananse decides to gather all the wisdom of the earth and keep it for himself. So he goes around collecting it, putting all of it into an earthen pot. When the pot is full, Ananse prepares to carry it to a treetop where no one else can find it. Holding the pot in front of him, he starts to climb. His son, Ntikuma, hides behind some bushes and then stepping out, calls his father.

"Father, may I make a suggestion?" The question only makes Ananse angry.

"Why are you spying on me?" he asks angrily.

"I want to help," Ntikuma says. "When you climb a tree, it is very hard to carry a pot in front of you. Put the pot on your back and you will be able to climb more easily."

Ananse puts the pot on his back and climbs, but he is embarrassed. Without his son's help he would not have known how to carry it. He is so embarrassed that he throws the pot down so that it shatters into many pieces when it hits the ground.

When people hear what has happened, they come and take some of the wisdom Ananse has thrown away. Today, wisdom is everywhere. Should you find a foolish man, he is one who did not come when the others took a share of the wisdom. (A variant of this story appears in Courlander, 1947, p. 587.)

Thus, in stories from the Old World, Ananse is sometimes a greedy fellow, not above tricking others to get what he wants. In spite of this weakness, he deserves respect. In a tale reminiscent of "The Five Chinese Brothers" (Bishop, 1938), Ananse's sons, members of the Dahomean and Yoruba pantheons of the gods, use magic to protect him.

HOW ANANSE WAS RESCUED BY HIS SONS

Kwaku Ananse, the Ashanti god, was in trouble. His son, See Trouble, who can see at a great distance, comes to his father's rescue when the father falls into the water. Then the father is swallowed by a fish, and Game Skinner, the third son, cuts open the fish to save his father. When a falcon steals Ananse, Stone Thrower, the fourth son, brings father back to earth with a stone. Cushion, the fifth son, then catches the father as he falls. Last of all, Road Builder brings all of them home on a road he constructs. (McDermott [1972] retells a version of this story in *Anansi the Spider.*)

ANANSI IN THE NEW WORLD

The slaves brought numerous stories to the New World and continued to tell them, in time changing them in a variety of ways. Sometimes they changed Anansi himself from a god to a spider, a man, or a man with spiderlike appendages. In Africa he was a rival of the high gods, an advocate for humankind; in the New World he often was in combat with powerful neighbors like Tiger, who, like the White masters, was a powerful, dangerous enemy. But like the slaves, Anansi himself was powerless. His success against great odds was a subtle guide for their survival (Jekyll, 1907). In one story from the Caribbean he takes on the powerful Tiger, who wants to go to war with him.

TIGER AND ANANCY MEET FOR WAR

Tiger sends a message saying that he is coming round to Anancy's house to kill him. So some time later Tiger comes on horseback with weapons and an army of friends.

"I have come to fight," Tiger calls across the fence. "Come out here." But Anancy refuses. He is waiting with one other friend in his yard, and he has no weapons.

"No. You must come to me," calls Anancy from the yard.

Tiger's friends are puzzled. They wonder what trick Anancy will play. Bro Tiger gives his weapons to his men and comes into the yard saying, "I have come to shake your hand. I want all the world to know that we are good, good friends."

Still Anancy only says, "Go away. I am not your friend."

Tiger steps through the yard gate and sinks into a pit concealed by dry leaves—with rocks at the bottom. The Tiger men rush up to the pit and try to get Bro Tiger out. At last he is lifted out, all battered, his legs broken.

Anancy and his friend Dog see none of this. They have gone about their business.

In this and many other stories in which Anansi takes on powerful enemies, he shows that he (and the African-Americans) is brave and can survive
in a hostile world where he is weak and has few advantages. (As with Anansi, so with the African-Americans.)

Many of the stories so popular with blacks in the New World are variants of ones which first appeared in Africa. Always, stories from Africa
were adapted to fit the new situation. A favorite story that has many variants both in Africa and America is about Anansi (or sometimes Bre'r Rabbit in America; see Harris, 1987) and how he steals food from a field. In
Africa the field belongs to Nyame, the sky god; in the New World, to Tiger
or sometimes to Asa, Anansi's wife.

But, even though they are different from each other, the stories are alike
in a variety of ways. In all of them Anansi decides to steal food even though
the villagers will consider it a crime. Anansi is always too stupid to tell that
the "tar baby," "tar board" or "tar creature" is just that. And he is always
punished. Sometimes he gets a sound beating; sometimes he is shamed in
front of all the people in the village and changes quickly from man to spider.
Then he hides in the corner of the ceiling, where he is to be found to this
day. Whatever the ending of the story, Anansi is always punished one way
or another, thus providing listeners with a cautionary tale. The following
variant is from the island of St. Croix:

BRER NANCY AND THE TAR BOARD

As a favor, Brer Nancy plants a field of yam for Tiger. But when it is
ripe and time to dig it up, he wants some pay. He decides to steal
some and hide it in his house. Tiger is angry about the theft. He covers two pieces of wood with tar and puts the tar board in the middle
of the field.

Thinking that he has found someone else stealing from the field,
Brer Nancy sneaks up to the board and hits it with his hand. Naturally, his hand sticks. Naturally, also, try as he may, he cannot free it.

So, he hits it with the other hand. Naturally, it also sticks and he
cannot free it. He stands there for a long time unable to move. Finally,
in anger, he butts it with his head, which also sticks. Try as he may,
he cannot free it.

There he sits stuck to the tar board for three full days. On the
third day a cock comes by and Brer Nancy calls for help, but the bird
refuses to rescue him. So Brer Nancy sits and sits there all alone.

Then Brer Nancy sees a bull passing. He begs for help, but the
bull will have nothing to do with him. So he sits there and sits there
all alone.

Finally, a ram goat passes by. Brer Nancy asks him for help. This time, Brer Nancy is lucky. The ram goat agrees to help. The goat moves back from the tar board and runs as fast as it can toward the tar board fastening his own head and jerking Brer Nancy free at the same time.

Brer Nancy kills the ram goat, slashes off the ram skin from the carcass and carries it home. (A variant of this appears in Courlander, 1947, p. 113.)

But in spite of the price he always pays, Anansi continues tricking people. In the next story, from the Caribbean, he wants to get a meal at a birthday party that he goes to even though he knows he is likely to be unwelcome.

ANANSI AND THE BIRTHDAY PARTIES

For his birthday feast Anansi invites all the animals in the forest. Although he is not invited, Tortoise also comes. Anansi tries to get rid of him by telling everyone to wash their hands in the creek. Tortoise goes to wash his hands, but they are dirtied again on the way back from the stream. So he does not eat at the table that day.

Soon afterwards Tortoise has a birthday, too. Because he knows that Anansi is light and cannot come under water, he decides to have the party underwater. Because he wants to go to the party, Anansi borrows a pair of breeches and a coat to wear and places stones in his coat pockets.

When Tortoise sees what Anansi has done, he tells all the guests to take off their coats. Anansi, of course, immediately floats to the top and so he does not get any food to eat. Greed caused this to happen to him. (A version of this appears in Courlander, 1947, p. 215.)

Perhaps Anansi learned that people get even when other people trick them, but probably not. In one Caribbean story, he even tricks his wife because he wants her to make him some chicken soup with her six chickens. When she refuses, he pretends to be sick and about to die.

MR NANCY AND THE CHICKEN SOUP

Mr. Nancy is sick, sick. He say he going to die, so his wife say she will go to the doctor for a cure, cure. After she leaves the house, she looks back and sees Anansi rushing off in the opposite direction. She follow him and he go right to the doctor's house. There she see him talking to Bro Dog. The two go into the house and when she knock, a "doctor" with a heavy beard greet her. He tell her to give her husband chicken soup to cure him.

She hurry home to help him, but when she get there, she find that Mr. Nancy is no longer sick. He is up and about making a great pot of soup with her now-dead chickens. To get even, she invites the whole village to have a dinner of chicken soup. (A variant of this appears in Berry, 1988, p. 54.)

Although Anansi may love tricks, he sometimes is merely silly. In some stories he is so silly that audiences sometimes laugh even before they hear his tale. In one Jamaican story he longs for a wife so much that he is positive that all sorts of unlikely choices seem right for him.

ANANSI IN LOVE

Anansi is in love. He falls in love with a mass of red flowers waving in the breeze, with a rainbow in the sky, with the clouds floating past him. Then he suddenly hears a small crackling sound. Flickering before his eyes is a tiny flame. He walks around Flame admiring and saying, "Hello, hello, hello." Flame echoes what he says, "Hell-o-o-o."

The flame echoes everything he says, and that is enough for Anansi. Excited, he asks her to visit him the next day. "Will you come?" "Yes, I wi-i-l-l if you prepare a special path for me-e-e."

"Tell me what to do. I will do anything you ask."

"This is what you d-o-o-o. Put down dry leaves, twigs, and grass along the way to your house. I will c-o-o-me."

Anansi dances around Flame and runs off to gather twigs, grass, and leaves for the visit. As he goes, he sings,

> I'm happy; I'm happy.
> Flame will be my wife.
> I'm happy; I'm happy.
> I'll have her all my life.

He works all afternoon and well into the night placing dry twigs, grass, and sticks on a narrow path through the woods and the pasture, through the village, to the front door of his house. When he finally goes to sleep, he looks forward to the big day.

In the morning he awakens with the sun and sings while he waits for Flame. But he has a long wait.

After many hours, Anansi spies Flame moving slowly but steadily toward his house, but she is no little Flame. One look at the huge, roaring blaze and Anansi backs up against his house in terror. Rumbling while approaching and eating up everything on the path, Flame leaps toward him with a menacing thrust. Quickly, Anansi sweeps the path of dry leaves away from his house toward the babbling brook flowing down the hill from his house. Flame follows the path leading her into the water. Sputtering and spitting, she gets smaller with each hiss. Then she is gone. From that day forward, Anansi never makes the same mistake. (A similar story appears in Berry, 1988, p. 1.)

Recent stories from the Caribbean sometimes show a more responsible Anansi. No longer the fool, on occasion he is concerned about the welfare of others. In one tale he tries to save the life of his friend, Bro Dog, when Bro Tiger endangers the friend's life.

ANANCY SAVES A FRIEND

It is holiday time and everyone is eating and drinking, having fun. Anancy has more than one drink, but Bro Dog has many more. The truth is, he is tipsy and he is a big show-off. He brags that he has more sense than anyone else.

"Maybe you have more senses than anyone else," says Anancy.

Bro Dog agrees with him. "I am sure that I have more senses than anyone. I think I have eleven. My nose is one; my mouth is another, my legs are two and my voice is another."

"So you have eleven senses."

"Yes," says Bro Dog.

"I have only two," says Anancy.

"I feel sorry for you."

"Yes," Anancy goes on. "I know myself and I know my friend."

The next morning Anancy finds Tiger getting ready to eat Bro Dog, whom he is holding in one hand.

"Bro Tiger," Anancy says, "you sure have a great meal there. You should make the sign of the cross in thanks for the meal before you eat."

Bro Tiger is mixed up. He does not like looking stupid. He lets go of Bro Dog and makes a sign of the cross. Bro Dog runs quick, quick and hides. Just as quick, quick Bro Anancy turns into a spider and scurries up a tree, where he is hidden in the branches. (A version of this appears in Courlander, 1947, p. 113.)

In another tale Anansi comes to the rescue of a kidnapped child.

MRS. DOG, FIRST CHILD, AND MONKEY MOTHER

Mrs. Dog, a friend of Anansi, has many puppies, but Swing-Swing Janey is the cleverest. She can leap on to the low branches of a tree; she can catch a ball or a coconut with her front paws, and she can stand on her head. Everyone in town knows Swing-Swing Janey and admires her.

One day when the puppy is outside playing all alone, a mother monkey and her monkey children stop to watch her and lure her away. When Mrs. Dog calls her, the mother cannot find her anywhere, but one of the animals in the neighborhood remembers that Swing-Swing Janey left with the monkey family.

Mrs. Dog starts looking for her everywhere. Finally a man in a canoe tells her that he saw her with the monkeys. Mrs. Dog finds the family in the monkey village, but the monkey mother claims that Swing-Swing is not around.

Just then Swing-Swing appears and Mrs. Monkey grabs her and hides her in the monkey house before Mrs. Dog sees her. Suddenly, all the monkey aunts and uncles, fathers and mothers, brothers and sisters appear chattering, "Go home, clear out. Don't come back." Mrs. Dog leaves, her tail between her legs. On the way back she meets Anansi and Mr. Dog.

"I think Swing-Swing is with Mrs. Monkey."

"Where?"

"In her house. The monkeys all scared me away."

That is all Anansi needs. He goes to the monkey rocks and greets Mrs. Monkey.

"Hello, Mrs. Monkey. How are you today? Can you help me? I am looking for people who can do tricks."

"I can do lots of tricks," says Mrs. Monkey and she proves it by swinging from a tree while holding on to a branch with her tail. Anansi claps and laughs.

"Excellent. Do you also know the barking trick?"

"Sure," she says, but she cannot.

"Well," says Anansi raising his voice and shouting very loudly. "Is there anyone else here who can do the barking trick? If so, bark right now."

"There is no one," says Mrs. Monkey. But they all hear the sound of barking from far away. Mrs. Monkey jumps down from the tree, her head hung low in shame because she had lied. She goes to the house and lets Swing-Swing out. The puppy and her mother and father are happy because the Dog family are together again. (A version of this story appears in Berry, 1988, p. 72.)

ANANSI THE TRICKSTER: HERO FOR ALL SEASONS

This brief survey has outlined only a few of the changes in Anansi's personality. More than many other tricksters, he has changed in ways that reflect the fortunes and beliefs of the storytellers. Anansi's transformations, his changeability from story to story, his combination of good and bad and of laughter and trickery have been assets for the people who told and still tell his stories. He is a hero for all seasons.

REFERENCES

Berry, J. (1988). *Spiderman Anancy*. New York: Holt.

Bishop, C. H. (1938). *The five Chinese brothers*. Illustrated by Kurt Wiese. New York: Coward, McCann & Geoghegan.

Brathwaite, E. K. (1971). *Folk culture of the slaves in Jamaica*. London: New Beacon.

Clarkson, A., & Cross, G. B. (1980). *World folktales*. New York: Scribner's.

Courlander, R. (1947). *Cow-tail switch*. New York: Holt.

Dance, D. C. (1985). *Folklore from contemporary Jamaicans*. Knoxville: University of Tennessee Press.

Haley, G. E. (1970). *A story, a story*. New York: Atheneum.

Harris, J. C. (1987). *Jump again! More adventures of Brer Rabbit*. San Diego: Harcourt Brace Jovanovich.

McDermott, G. (1972). *Anansi the spider*. New York: Holt.

Jekyll, W. (Ed.) (1907). *Jamaican song and story*. Introduction by Alice Werner. London: Folklore Society/Nutt.

RESOURCES FOR CHILDREN

Aardema, V. (1984). *Oh Kojo, how could you!* Illustrated by Marc Brown. New York: Dial.

Appiah, P. (1966). *Ananse the Spider. Tales from an Ashanti village*. New York: Pantheon.

Bryan, A. (1971). *The ox of the wonderful horns and other African folktales*. New York: Atheneum.

Kimmel, E. (1988). *Anansi and the moss-covered rock*. Illustrated by Janet Stevens. New York: Holiday House.

Kirn, A. (Reteller). (1968). *Beeswax catches a thief*. New York: Norton.

Mohan, B. (Reteller). (1964). *Punia and the king of sharks*. Illustrated by Don Bolognese. Chicago: Follett.

Roche, A. K. (1969). *The clever turtle*. Englewood Cliffs, NJ: Prentice Hall.

TRY THIS

Tell or read Anansi stories to your pupils. Some should be from Africa, others from the New World. After you have finished, encourage the boys and girls to compare the stories.

1. Who are Anansi's rivals in the New World? In Africa?
2. Why does he trick others? Is he sometimes greedy? Does he ever act in a thoughtful fashion? Does he help anyone?
3. Does he act in a silly fashion?
4. Is there a difference between the way he acted in Africa and the ways he acts in the New World?

A matrix similar to the one in the "Try This" at the end of chapter 10 can be used to help children during this discussion. Next compare other tricksters with Anansi.

When the students have discussed a number of tricksters, ask them each to choose their favorite, draw a picture, and tell a story that they themselves make up about him. Later, create a class book of the trickster stories and their pictures.

—*G.B.*

CHAPTER 12

NOTES FROM A JEWISH STORYTELLER

Eric A. Kimmel

The panorama of Jewish folklore is the topic of the next chapter by
Eric Kimmel, popular storyteller, professor of children's literature,
and author of a number of children's books, including *Hershel and
the Hanukkah Goblins* and *The Chanukkah Tree*. In this engaging
chapter, Professor Kimmel introduces us to the sources he used to
write *Hershel and the Hanukkah Goblins* and the changes he made
to meet American children's needs and experiences. In the process
we gain insight into the way authors often adapt folktales for their
own purposes.

> *"Iz gevayn a mool a maylekh . . ."*
> "Once upon a time there was a king . . ."

And so my grandmother would begin another story. She knew hundreds.
As we sorted seeds for the garden or sat by the back window watching the
snow fall, she led me through a magic landscape where Moses and Solomon
lived alongside imps of the Slavic forest, where Kaisers Wilhelm and Franz
Josef and Czar Nicholas II were as real as Ashmodai, king of the demons,
or that irrepressible trickster, Hershel of Ostropol.

I was more fortunate than many of my friends. My grandmother lived
with us, so I grew up speaking Yiddish, specifically the broad Galician dialect that lends itself so well to storytelling. When I started school it was
accepted as a matter of course that I would also attend Hebrew school,
which I did for three days a week and a half-day on Sunday until the time I
left home to go to college. This was a real school with trained teachers. We
studied Bible, liturgy, Hebrew language and literature, and Jewish history.
Here was a story 4,000 years old that was as much a part of me as I was
part of it. This is where I first became acquainted with such outstanding
writers as Chaim Nachman Bialik, Y. L. Peretz, Sholom Aleichem, and the
Singer brothers, Israel Joshua and Isaac Bashevis.

Consequently, I think it far from accidental or even surprising that I became a teller and a writer of tales from the Jewish folkloric tradition. There is a Chinese saying, "Give a man a fish and you feed him for a day; teach him to fish and you feed him for a lifetime." The expanse of Jewish lore fills an ocean. The storyteller who knows how to navigate its reefs and currents can never fail to bring up a full net.

To begin with, there is Torah. This is the Pentateuch, the Five Books of Moses: Genesis, Exodus, Leviticus, Numbers, and Deuteronomy. Torah plus the writings of Prophets (*Nevi'im*) and Chronicles (*Ketuvim*) makes up the *Tanakh,* otherwise known as the Bible or Old Testament. Bible, and especially Torah, forms the core of the Jewish faith and lies at the heart of its folk literature. Not only the characters, but more important, the attitudes and understandings about human beings, their ties to their fellow creatures, their relationship to the universe, and the Creator Who brought it into being stem from Torah. As an example, consider the following comparison between Noah and Abraham, taken from rabbinical traditions.

> Why does the Torah say that Noah was a righteous man in his generation whereas of Abraham it only says that he was a righteous man? This is because Noah appears righteous only in contrast to the people of his time. Had he lived at another time, he would not be considered righteous. Abraham, however, would have been regarded as righteous in any age. How do we know this? When the Lord told Noah He would bring a flood to destroy the earth, Noah accepted it without comment. On the other hand, when Abraham learned the Lord intended to destroy the Cities of the Plain, he pleaded for the lives of the inhabitants, although he knew there weren't ten good people among them. (*Sanhedrin*, p. 108)

Midrash is second to Torah and Tanakh as a prime source of stories. The Midrashim are an ancient body of writings expanding and expounding on the biblical text. Tales from the Midrash, while not possessing the authority of scripture, nonetheless offer surprising insights into the personalities of biblical figures. Let us use the following story about the Patriarch Abraham as an example (Glen, 1929).

> Abraham was renowned for his hospitality. No wayfarer was ever turned away from his tent. One day an elderly traveller appeared. Abraham washed his feet, brought him food and drink, and invited him to stay as his guest. After eating, the old man took an idol from his belongings and began worshipping it. The thought that a guest would abuse his hospitality by worshipping idols in his home sent Abraham into a fury. He drove the old man out into the desert. That evening the Lord spoke to Abraham: "Abraham, where is the old man I sent you?"

"He was an idol worshipper. I drove him out into the desert."

"Abraham, Abraham," the Lord said, "that old man is eighty years old. I have been patient with him for eighty years. Could you not be patient with him for one night?"

Ashamed, Abraham went at once into the desert. He found the old man and, begging his forgiveness, invited him back to his tent with permission to worship whatever gods he pleased. The old man stayed in Abraham's encampment. In time he came to believe in the True God and put aside his idols. (p. 60)

Aggadah is similar to Midrash, except that Aggadic tales are drawn from the Talmud, the body of commentary and discussion on Jewish law compiled in Israel and Babylon (Iraq) from the third to the sixth century C.E. It is hard to generalize about Aggadah because, like the Talmud, it appears to flow in many directions at once. There are stories about famous rabbis such as fierce Shammai, gentle Hillel, and fantastic characters such as Resh Lakish, a former brigand who fought as a gladiator in the Roman arena. There are tales that rabbis tell about other rabbis, fables and folktales used to illustrate a point or illuminate a discussion, as well as random stories only loosely connected to the matter at hand. This tale is told about Rabbi Hillel, who was famous for his gentleness and patience (Ausubel, 1960).

There was great animosity between Jews and Greeks during the Roman period. A Greek once wagered his companions four hundred silver drachmas that he could make Hillel angry. He pounded on Hillel's door on Friday afternoon. Hillel was bathing in preparation for the Sabbath. He wrapped himself in a towel and opened the door.

"What do you want, my friend?" he asked the Greek.

"I have a question," the man said. "Why do Babylonians have round skulls?"

Hillel answered, "Because their midwives are unskilled."

The man went away, only to come back a few minutes later. Once again he pounded on Hillel's door.

"Hillel! Come out! I have another question."

Hillel wrapped himself in the towel again and opened the door. "Did you want to speak to me?"

"Yes. I want to know why the Africans have broad feet."

"That is because they live in swampy or sandy places," Hillel answered. "Do you have any more questions?"

"Yes, I have many questions," the man replied. "But I am afraid to ask them because you may get angry."

Hillel smiled. "Don't be afraid. Ask me as many questions as you like."

The man frowned. "Do you know you have cost me 400 silver drachmas?"

"How so?"

"Because I wagered I could make you angry."

Hillel shook his head. He said to the man, "Better you should lose 400 silver drachmas than I should lose my temper." (pp. 106–107, *paraphrased*)

Bible, Midrash, and Aggadah form the roots and trunk of the tree of Jewish folktales. The leaves and branches are as varied as the places where Jews have settled. Some "Jewish" tales are in fact stories from other lands retold by Jewish tellers, but with little identifiable Jewish content. This process of cultural interchange and transmission has been going on for over a thousand years. In the Middle Ages, when the boundary between the Christian West and the Muslim Middle East was a battlefront, Jewish storytellers served as a conduit through which "Sinbad the Sailor" and other tales from the Islamic world first entered Europe.

I recently had a personal experience with this type of cross-cultural exchange. In 1976 I published a collection of stories based on my grandmother's tales in a book entitled *Mishka, Pishka, and Fishka* (Kimmel, 1976). One of the stories, "Death and Baba Tsigan," was about an encounter between an old gypsy woman and Death. I had to piece it together from the few fragments I remembered. It is an unusual story, one I have never found anywhere else, which led me to assume it was one my grandmother made up. To my surprise, I received a letter from Ted Potochniak, a Canadian-Ukrainian writer and storyteller, asking permission to include elements of my story in a version he was contributing to a collection of favorite stories by Canadian storytellers. It appears his Ukrainian grandmother told him the same story, or at least one similar to it, when he was a boy. So is this a Jewish story or a Ukrainian story? I tend to think it's primarily the latter. My grandmother spoke Ukrainian and had warm friendships with Ukrainian people. Think then, of the travels of this one tale. My grandmother as a child hears it in Ukrainian; 60 years later she tells it to me in Yiddish; 20 years later I write it in English; 10 years later it is reunited with its Ukrainian counterpart in Canada, and possibly retold in Ukrainian. And yet for at least three generations it has been a story told by Jews.

It is no accident, therefore, that a reader going through a collection of Jewish folktales will find Sephardic tales whose form and content mirror the *Arabian Nights* or Ashkenazic tales that bear more than a passing resemblance to stories in Grimm and Afanas'ev. If that is the case, what makes a story "Jewish?"

TRUE JEWISH THEMES

It is not a matter of language or geography, but one of theme. A truly Jewish story will exhibit thematic elements that do not ordinarily appear in stories from other cultures. Most prominent will be the theme of Loss and Exile, of Redemption being so near and yet so far. *It is said that if all the Jews in the world would faithfully observe one Sabbath, the Messiah would come.* The Prophet Elijah frequently appears in disguise. Legend pictures the guardians of Israel—King David sleeping in his tomb, Abraham waiting on a desert island—waiting to rise up and free their people. But the time has not yet come, as shown in the following tale about Rabbi Wolf Kitzes and the Baal Shem Tov (Buber, 1958).

> Before Rabbi Wolf Kitzes set out on a sea voyage, his teacher, Rabbi Israel Baal Shem Tov, warned him, "Think before you speak."
>
> It was a terrible voyage. Rabbi Wolf's ship was wrecked on a desert island. All aboard were lost, with the exception of Rabbi Wolf, who found himself cast up on an uninhabited shore. He wandered about the island in a vain search for food. When he was on the point of giving up, he encountered an ancient man dressed in shining garments. The man led him to a table set with a sumptuous feast. "This is for you. Eat your fill," he told Rabbi Wolf. Before Rabbi Wolf started eating, the man asked, "How does it fare with my people Israel?" Rabbi Wolf muttered a quick reply. "The Lord does not desert them."
>
> Later the man led him to the other side of the island. A ship sailed by. Rabbi Wolf hailed it. Thus he was rescued and completed his journey. When he returned home, he told Rabbi Israel about his strange adventure. The Baal Shem smote his breast with sorrow.
>
> "Did I not caution you to think before you spoke? The ancient man on the island was our Father, Abraham. Every day he asks the Lord, 'How fares my people Israel?' Every day the Lord answers, 'I do not desert them.' Why did you not tell him about the Exile?" (pp. 63–64, *paraphrased*)

A second important characteristic of authentically Jewish tales is that the hero is usually a religious figure, or at the very least a morally conscious individual. The close presence of God is a frequent element in these stories. The wicked are punished and the just are rewarded, usually after undergoing terrible sufferings by which their faith and moral integrity are tested. Another pattern involves a character who learns through the intercession of an angel or the Prophet Elijah that seemingly unjust occurrences are in fact manifestations of divine justice. Even tricksters such as Hershel Ostropolier and his Galician counterpart Froym Graydiger are at heart profoundly moral individuals, a significant difference from other tricksters—Anansi, Coyote, Till Eulenspiegel—whose physical and sensual appetites are boundless. It remains, however, a Jewish morality.

This was brought home to me on one occasion when I was asked to appear as a guest speaker at a Young Author's conference at a local school. I told several Hershel of Ostropol tales, including the well-known one, "What His Father Did" (Ausubel, 1960).

> Hershel stopped one night at an inn. Since he had no money, he begged the innkeeper for a meal. The innkeeper refused. Hershel flew into a rage. He grabbed the innkeeper and shook him back and forth, shouting, "If you don't give me something to eat, I'll do what my father did!" Naturally the innkeeper didn't want to find out what that was, so he emptied the larder and invited Hershel to eat his fill. Afterwards, he timidly asked Hershel what it was that his father did. Hershel replied, "When my father didn't get anything to eat . . . he went to bed hungry." (p. 313, *paraphrased*)

During the question-and-answer portion of the talk, one of the parents challenged my judgment in presenting that story. She felt it was an immoral tale. After all, she noted, Hershel could have offered to work in exchange for a meal. This was an eye-opening moment for me; the Protestant ethic colliding head-on with the Jewish worldview. The questioner's reaction was justified, considering the story from her frame of reference. One of the hallmarks of Calvinist belief is, work hard, save your money, be honest and upright, and prosperity will follow. Material prosperity is the outward manifestation of spiritual grace, and those who fall short in most cases have only themselves to blame. In contrast, the Jewish view holds that prosperity ultimately comes from God and that only a sliver of divine favor, not necessarily earned, stands between the magnate and the pauper (What does God think of money? Look who he gives it to!). The well-to-do therefore have the responsibility of caring for the poor. In addition, the act of giving charity is a *mitzvah,* the act of fulfilling a divine command. Thus, within the Jewish context, the innkeeper is plainly being immoral by not offering a hungry man food. Hershel tricks him, as well he should, but only out of what should have been given freely.

This emphasis on an ethical morality coupled with a constant affirmation of the social contract is perhaps the most distinctive quality of Jewish tales. Not even God is immune from responsibility. In a famous, though perhaps mythical, Yom Kippur sermon, the saintly Hasidic rabbi Levi Yitzchak of Berdichev took God to task for the condition of the Jewish masses.

"Maybe Israel hasn't measured up, but if you think gentiles can do better, *loz Ivan blizen shoifar!*" Let Ivan blow the ram's horn! In a similar vein the Dubno Maggid, a noted preacher, took his friend the learned and aristocratic Vilna Gaon to task. "You sit in your study; you read all the holy books; you follow all the laws down to the last detail. Come out of your study. Descend into the marketplace with the people. Live as they live, endure what they endure. Then we will see how long you will remain the Vilna Gaon."

For a people supposedly obsessed with money—which is how the Jew is invariably depicted in every folk tradition from Ireland to Persia—accumulating wealth plays little role in the stories Jews tell each other. Jewish folk heroes are much more likely to be paupers than millionaires. Discussions of wealth, on the few occasions when they appear, tend to be ironic, especially since the main character in these stories is usually a *melamed.* The melamed taught small children their letters. It was a low-paying, marginal profession, the last refuge for the incompetent, unmotivated, and unskilled.

> Two melameds were talking. "Oy," said one, "if only I were as rich as Rothschild!"
> "Hah!" the other said. "Rothschild isn't so smart. If I were Rothschild, I'd be richer than Rothschild!"
> "How could anyone be richer than Rothschild?"
> "I'd teach a few students on the side." (Oral tradition)

These hapless teachers are close cousins of characters who are staples of Jewish folklore. These are the *shlemiel,* the Sad Sack who can't do anything right, and the *shlimazel,* Mr. Bad Luck.

The origin of the word *shlemiel* is obscure. One theory attributes it to a certain Shlumiel who returned from a journey of 11 months to find his wife had given birth to a child. Suspicious, but not overly bright, he went to the rabbi for confirmation that the baby was in fact his. The rabbi, a compassionate man, searched the Talmud and—sure enough—found evidence that an 11-month pregnancy was possible! Shlumiel believed it, and in doing so gave his name to generations of descendants. (Oral tradition)

> A *shadchan,* a professional matchmaker, was trying to arrange a match between a painfully shy shlemiel and an attractive young girl. The prospect of their first meeting unnerved the young man. "What do I say?" he asked the shadchan.
> "It's very simple. First you talk about love, to show her you have an affectionate heart. Then you talk about family, to prove you'll be a

reliable husband. Finally you talk about philosophy, to show you have an intellect."

At last the dreaded moment came when parents and shadchan left the room so the prospective couple could get acquainted.

"Do you love . . . *knaidelach* [dumplings]?" the young man began. That was love.

"I suppose so," the girl answered.

"Does your brother love knaidelach?" That was family.

"I don't have a brother."

Now for philosophy. "If you had a brother, would he love knaidelach?"

Shlimazel derives from a combination of the German *schlimm* ("bad") and the Hebrew *mazal* ("luck"). A classic definition of the two types is that the *shlemiel* is the waiter who spills soup into the lap of the *shlimazel*. If a shlimazel sold umbrellas, it would never rain again. If he made coffins, no one would ever die. (Ausubel, 1960)

A desperate shlimazel went to the bank. "Help me, I need a loan. If you don't give me a loan, I'll go into the hat business."

The banker laughed. "Is this a threat? Why should I care if you go into the hat business?"

"You don't understand," said the shlimazel. "When someone like me goes into the hat business, every child from now on will be born without a head!" (Ausubel, 1960, p. 347)

All of these elements come together in the Chelm stories. Chelm, the town of fools, is the microcosm of Jewish experience. Here the convolutions of Talmudic thought are carried to such extremes as to leave logic and even common sense behind. The Chelmers are not so much fools as they are prisoners of their own dialectic.

A Chelmer once went on a trip to Lemberg. While there, he stayed at an inn. The innkeeper, a jolly fellow, liked to entertain his guests with riddles. He said to the Chelmer, "Tell me who it is—he's my father's son, but he's not my brother."

The Chelmer racked his brains, but he couldn't think of an answer.

"It's me!" the innkeeper told him.

"That's a good riddle," the Chelmer said. When he got back to Chelm he shared it with his friends. "He's my father's son, but he's not my brother. Who is it?"

"We give up. Who?"

"It's the innkeeper in Lemberg." (Oral tradition)

Ironically, the real Chelm, a midsized Polish city, was a noted Talmudic center in the 17th century and the actual source of the golem legend. Contemporary accounts mention the kabbalist Elijah of Chelm as having brought a clay figure to life. Rabbi Judah Loeb of Prague does not enter into the tale until 200 years later. By then a town whose inhabitants reportedly attempted to capture the moon in a barrel of borscht and condemned a lobster to death by drowning could no longer be taken seriously.

JEWISH THEMES IN MY STORIES

One of the questions children always ask a visiting author is "What made you decide to become a writer?" In my case the decision goes back to elementary school. I had two wonderful teachers in the first and third grades, Mrs. McGroarty and Mrs. Miles. (Most of the children at P.S. 193 were Jewish, whereas most of the teachers were Irish Catholic. As a result I've always felt that the notion that children need teachers of their own ethnic background is nonsense. Sensitivity, positivity, and enthusiasm are infinitely more important for children's learning than a particular skin color or last name.) Our classrooms were filled with books. Mrs. McGroarty and Mrs. Miles read aloud every day, with great flair, and encouraged us to do the same. Learning to read was a great adventure, and not one of us doubted we would succeed, because it was so much fun. However, when Christmas rolled around, I invariably found myself cringing in my seat because the Hanukkah material brought in to balance the overwhelmingly Christian content of Santas, stockings, carols, and trees was so appallingly lame.

There are reasons for this. Hanukkah is a minor holiday. It is not mentioned in the Bible. No special service takes place in the synagogue. There is no significant body of liturgy or lore associated with it. Even the tale of the cruse of holy oil that burned for 8 days instead of one is a fabrication, promulgated by the rabbis to reinforce the belief that God, not the increasingly corrupt Hasmonean dynasty, was the true savior of Israel. As a result, there was no Jewish midwinter festival to compete with Christmas, so American Jews had to manufacture one. Hanukkah filled the bill. It fell at the right time of year, and it also had elements of decorations, colored lights, presents, and feasting that could be pumped up to make Jewish children feel as if they too had a holiday "to drive the cold winter away."

Our public school teachers tried their best. However, they were unfamiliar with Jewish sources, although even here there was not much to choose from. The heroic Macabbees, Sadie Rose Weilerstein's (1942) "K'ton-ton" stories and the dismal lyric "I Had a Little Dreidel" constituted all that was available. Our Hebrew school teachers didn't offer much more. However, they didn't feel compelled to do so. Within the Jewish context, the High Holidays; the agricultural festivals; Israel Independence Day; and raucous, noisy Purim were far more important than Hanukkah.

But most Jewish children in America don't live in an exclusively Jewish context, especially if they attend public school. Which led me to make a personal vow, long ago, that if I ever grew up and became an author—my secret ambition for years and years—I would endeavor to write a decent Hanukkah story. And not just for Jewish children.

It came to pass. I did become a writer; many of my stories have Jewish themes and many of them are Hanukkah tales. I see myself not as a folklorist but as a storyteller; one familiar with Jewish sources but not limited to or by them. The majority of my books are actually collages of material drawn from several different traditions and placed in new settings. *The Chanukkah Tree* (Kimmel, 1976) is a good example. It began on a rainy morning in March with a radio report on the Oregon economy. The Christmas tree growers, one of our state's major industries, had had a bad year. I thought of all those beautiful trees tossed into a landfill. That's when the wheels started turning. If someone had a Christmas tree to sell, but everyone who needed a tree had already bought one, then one would have to find another market. Why not Jews? But Jewish people wouldn't buy a Christmas tree. It would have to be repackaged as . . . a Hanukkah tree. Now who would be dumb enough to fall for that? The people of Chelm, naturally! Here was a story, but the story didn't have an end until my wife suggested putting birds into it. Her passion is birdwatching, and her answer for every problem is to put in a bird. So I added birds, and it worked.

Hershel and the Hanukkah Goblins (Kimmel, 1976) was put together the same way. I've loved Hershel of Ostropol since the days when I squatted in the backyard pulling out weeds while my grandmother told one Hershel story after another. I had recently finished rereading Afanas'ev's classic collection of Russian tales and still had one of my favorites, "Ivanko, the Bear's Son," in mind. In that story a woman is kidnapped by a bear and has a child by him. The boy is a bear from the waist down and a human being from the waist up. After the woman escapes from the bear and takes Ivanko home, her husband gives Ivanko several tasks in the hope of getting rid of him. One is to make a goblin pay rent. I gave Hershel Ivanko's tasks, multiplied the goblins by eight, and I had a story. Thinking of weird goblins and ways to fool them was easy, but working out the climax was the difficult part. In the story, the king of the goblins has to light the Hanukkah candles himself. That is the only way for Ivanko to break his power. The confrontation between Hershel and the goblin king has to be convincing within the context of the tale and the two characters. If it appears contrived, the story failed. The key to the ending came from a pamphlet on street crime. The mugger has the advantage over his victim because he has the scenario worked out. He knows what he's going to do, and he has a fairly good idea what his victim will do. If the victim refuses to play along, however, the plan falls apart. The mugger has to improvise, and that's the point where a clever victim can seize the initiative and turn the tables. The king of the goblins intends to destroy Hershel, but first Hershel has to cringe and beg for his life. The king, like most bullies, has a fragile ego. But Hershel refuses to play along. He doesn't beg; he isn't defiant—the goblin king is prepared for those possibilities—he does the unexpected. He refuses to acknowledge the threat exists. "You can't fool me. You're one of the boys from the village!" The king of the goblins loses sight of his main purpose and allows himself to be sidetracked into trying to convince Hershel that he really exists (Figure 12.1). Hershel, by seizing the initiative, tricks the king into lighting the candles himself. End of goblins. End of story.

But not the end of controversy. The reaction to *The Chanukkah Tree* surprised me. I expected criticism from the Orthodox press, but they loved it. The most scathing reviews I received came from the liberal side. I was accused of being everything from a "Jews for Jesus" freak to making fun of people who choose to have a Hanukkah bush in their homes. One irate individual pointed to the book and sputtered, "You can't do that! You can't mix Christmas and Hanukkah!" As if we don't live in a country where it's already done.

Hershel and the Hanukkah Goblins caught its share of criticism, too. Countless people have told me "We don't have goblins in our religion." Not so. Jewish literature going back to the time of the Talmud abounds with tales of imps and devils, spirits and exorcisms. Why did my grandmother teach me to kiss the mezuzah on the bedroom door and say a little prayer every night before I went to bed, and why did she nearly have a fit when she caught my brother and me making shadow figures on a wall? Of course, we didn't call them goblins. They were *shaydim,* which more properly translates as demons, devils, or imps. But "goblins" isn't too far afield. Actually the story was originally titled "Hershel and the Hanukkah Demons" when Marianne Carus accepted it for the December, 1985, issue of *Cricket.* Knowing the problems Marianne has with fundamentalists, I suggested she change the title to "Hershel and the Hanukkah Goblins," which actually works better. Shaydim are traditionally creatures of darkness who

Figure 12.1   Hershel tricks a goblin in *Hershel and
the Hanukkah Goblins*

dwell in ruins. They exist because they fulfill a divine purpose. In the Jewish
faith Satan is humanity's adversary, not God's.

I am happy that these stories have been well received because they were
written for all children. I want non-Jewish children to hear about Hershel
and Chelm as much as I want Jewish children to know about *A Christmas
Carol, The Night Before Christmas,* and *A Child's Christmas in Wales*. Both
traditions are part of our cultural heritage as human beings and belong, as
such, to people everywhere.

REFERENCES

Deriving references from this chapter was a task that had to be accomplished after the fact, because I have known most of these stories from childhood. In those instances where I was unable to find a written source for a story, I ascribed it to the oral tradition, although I am sure that texts exist somewhere for all of them. The following titles will be useful for anyone interested in learning more about Jewish traditional tales:

Afanes'ev, A. (1973). *A treasury of Jewish folklore*. New York: Pantheon.

Ben Gorian, M. J. (1976). *Mimekor Yisrael* (Vols. 1–3). Bloomington: Indiana University Press.

Buber, M. (1958). *Tales of the Hasidim*. New York: Schocken.

Folklore. In *Encyclopedia Judaica* (Vol. 6, pp. 1374–1410). New York: Macmillan.

Glen, M. G. (1929). *Jewish tales and legends*. New York: Hebrew Publishing.

Kimmel, E. (1976). *Mishka, Pishka and Fishka and other Galician tales*. New York: Coward, McCann & Geoghegan.

Kimmel, E. (1989). *The Chanukkah tree*. New York: Holiday House.

Kimmel, E. (1989). *Hershel and the Hanukkah goblins*. New York: Holiday House.

Noy, D. (Ed.). (1963). *Folktales of Israel*. Chicago: University of Chicago Press.

Sadeh, P. (1989). *Jewish folktales*. New York: Anchor.

Schram, P. (1987). *Jewish stories one generation tells another*. Northvale, NJ: Aronson.

Schwartz, H. (1985). *Elijah's violin and other Jewish fairy tales*. New York: Harper Collins.

Schwartz, H. (1991a). *Lillith's cave: Jewish tales of the supernatural*. New York: Oxford University Press.

Schwartz, H. (1991b). *Miriam's tambourine: Jewish folktales from around the world*. New York: Oxford University Press.

Spalding, H. D. (Ed.). (1973). *Encyclopedia of Jewish humor*. Flushing, NY: Jonathan David.

Weilerstein, S. R. (1942). *What the moon brought*. Philadelphia: Jewish Publication Society.

Weinreich, B. S. (Ed.). (1988). *Yiddish folktales*. New York: Pantheon.

TRY THIS

Ask your children to compare Hershel of Ostropol in *Hershel and the Hanukkah Goblins* with other tricksters. Questions like the following will help children distinguish between him and other tricksters:

- Why does he trick the goblins?
- Is he greedy or generous?
- Is he funny or are the goblins the funny ones?
- Is Hershel clever?

(There is a difference between Hershel and other tricksters. Hershel tricks the goblins because he wants to make sure that the villagers will be able to celebrate Hanukkah. He is actually generous and clever. The goblins are silly and remarkably stupid.)

When the children have compared the stories, tell the class how Eric Kimmel changed the traditional story to fit the needs of American children, both Jewish and non-Jewish. Tell the class that authors often change folklore so that the stories fit today's world.

Next read another modern story like *Annie and the Old One* (Miles, 1971) to your class. Ask questions like:

- How does Annie trick her grandmother?
- Why did she change her mind?
- How is Annie different from the folklore tricksters?

(Annie tries to trick her grandmother because she is afraid that her grandmother will die when she finishes weaving a rug. We know from the story that she feels sorry for tricking her grandmother and that she has learned to accept the fact that her grandmother will die.)

During this discussion, continue adding to your matrix (see p. 000). Finally, ask your class how the two modern stories are different from traditional ones. Tell the children that folklore often does not focus on how people feel. Modern stories, on the other hand, do.

During the entire unit, have available other trickster stories like those listed below. When the children have had a chance to read a number of them, encourage the youngsters to make up their own trickster stories. Some of them may choose to update an old one. Others may prefer to make up an entirely new trickster story.

—G.B.

REFERENCES

Kimmel, E. (1989). *Hershel and the Hanukkah Goblins*. Illustrated by Trina Schart Hyman. New York: Holiday House.

Miles, Miska. (1971). *Annie and the Old One*. Illustrated by Peter Parnall. Boston: Little, Brown & Co.

BIBLIOGRAPHY

Selected List of Trickster Tales from Folklore

Appiah, P. (1966). How the pig got his snout. In *Ananse the spider*. New York: Pantheon.

Appiah, P. (1981). How Quaku Ananse became bald. In *Tales of an Ashanti father*. North Pomfret, VT: Deutsch.

Berg, L. (1966). The greedy spider. In *Folk tales for reading and telling*. North Pomfret, VT: Hodder and Stoughton.

Bierhorst, J. (1986). Rabbit and Coyote. In *The monkey's haircut and other tales told by the Maya*. New York: Morrow.

Brown, D. (1979). How Rabbit fooled Wolf, Coyote and the rolling rock, Skunk outwits Coyote. In *Tepee tales of the American Indians*. New York: Holt, Rinehart & Winston.

Bruchac, J. (1985). Turtle makes war on men. In *Iroquois stories*. Watsonville, CA: Crossing Press.

Clarkson, A., & Cross, G. (1986). Nasr-ed-Din Hodja in the pulpit. In *World folktales*. New York: Scribner's.

Cole, J. (Ed.). (1983). Brer Rabbit, businessman. In *Best loved folktales of the world*. New York: Doubleday.

Courlander, H. (1957a). Anansi and the elephant go hunting. In *The hat-shaking dance*. New York: Harcourt Brace Jovanovich.

Courlander, H. (1957b). Terrapin's pot of sense. In *Terrapin's pot of sense*. New York: Holt, Rinehart & Winston.

Courlander, H., & Herzog, G. (1947). Guinea Fowl and Rabbit get justice. In *The cow-tail switch and other West African stories*. New York: Holt, Rinehart & Winston.

Erdoes, R., & Ortiz, A. (1984). Adventures of Great Rabbit. In *American Indian myths and legends*. New York: Pantheon.

Goble, P. (1988). *Iktomi and the boulder*. New York: Orchard.

Goble, P. (1989). *Iktomi and the berries*. New York: Orchard.

Goble, P. (1990). *Iktomi and the ducks*. New York: Orchard.

Goble, P. (1991). *Iktomi and the buffalo skull*. New York: Orchard.

Green, M. (Ed.). (1965). The porcupine and the dog. In *The big book of animal fables*. New York: Franklin Watts, Inc.

Gringhuis, D. (1970). The racoon and the crawfish. In *Lore of the great turtle*. Mackinac City, MI: Mackinac Island State Park Commission.

Grinnell, G. B. (1962). *Blackfoot lodge tales.* Lincoln: University of Nebraska Press.

Haviland, V. (Ed.). (1965). The white hare and the crocodile. In *Favorite fairy tales told around the world.* Boston: Little, Brown.

Haviland, V. (Ed.). (1974). Wakaima and the clay man. In *The fairy tale treasury.* London: Penguin.

Haviland, V. (Ed.). (1979). Raven lets out the daylight. In *North American legends.* New York: Philomel.

Kimmel, E. (1989). *Hershel and the Hanukkah goblins.* Illustrated by Trina Schart Hyman. New York: Holiday House.

Leach, M. (1967). Why Spider has a little head and a big behind. In *How the people sang the mountain up.* New York: Viking.

Lester, J. (1987). Brer Rabbit gets caught one more time. In *The tales of Uncle Remus: The adventures of Brer Rabbit.* New York: Dial.

Lester, J. (1988). Brer Rabbit and Mr. Man's chickens. In *More tales of Uncle Remus: Further adventures of Brer Rabbit, his friends, enemies and others.* New York: Dial.

McDermott, G. (1973). *Anansi the spider.* New York: Holt, Rinehart & Winston.

Metayer, M. (1972). Kajortoq, the red fox. In *Tales from the igloo.* North Pomfret, VT: Hurtig.

Mieko, M. (1969). *How Rabbit tricked his friends.* New York: Parents Magazine Press.

Montgomerie, N. (Ed.). (1962). The rabbit and crocodile. In *To read and to tell.* London: Bodley Head.

Sturton, H. (1966). The great tug-of-war. In *Zomo the rabbit.* New York: Atheneum.

Uchida, Y. (Reteller). (1955). The fox and the bear. In *The magic listening cap: More folk tales from Japan.* New York: Harcourt Brace Jovanovich.

Walker, B. (1972). *How the hare told the truth about his horse.* New York: Parents Magazine Press.

Yolen, J. (Ed.). (1986). The Hodja and the cauldron. In *Favorite folktales from around the world.* New York: Pantheon.

Trickster Stories by Known Authors

Anderson, H. C. (1949). *The emperor's new clothes.* Illustrated by Virginia Lee Burton. Boston: Houghton Mifflin.

Hamilton, V. (1968). *The house of Dies Drear.* Illustrated by Eros Kieth. New York: Macmillan.

Kerr, M. E. (1972). *Dinky Hocker shoots smack.* New York: Harper & Row.

Miles, M. (1971). *Annie and the old one.* Boston: Atlantic-Little, Brown.

Mahy, M. (1986). *The tricksters.* New York: Macmillan.

Ness, E. (1966). *Sam, Bangs and moonshine.* New York: Holt, Rinehart & Winston.

Winthrop, E. (1985). *The castle in the attic.* New York: Holiday House.

CHAPTER 13

❀ HIGH FANTASIES:
SECRET OPENINGS TO THE RING OF MYTH

Gloria T. Blatt

In this chapter, G. T. Blatt, highlights an important connection between ancient myths and high fantasies, a form of fiction popular
among preadolescent and adolescent boys. Because this group of
boys often seems obsessed with quest stories, teachers can seize the
moment to introduce their charges to similar tales from the movies,
cartoons, ancient tales from Greece and Rome, and the northern
countries, thereby helping the youngsters to recognize an important
and common literary pattern in world literature.

My son Michael went through a period in the sixth through eighth grades
when he read one fantasy after another. He always seemed to have his head
in a book; and the books were always novels like *Taran Wanderer* (Alexander, 1967) or the *Dark Is Rising* (Cooper, 1973). He often talked about
Dungeons and Dragons, a game that he played in school and out. Clearly,
something in these books was speaking to him in an important way.

SOME REASONS FOR THE CHILDREN'S READING
PREFERENCES

I began to understand why he was so fascinated with fantasy when I
read a number of studies (Greenlaw & Wielan, 1979; Huus, 1964; Purves
& Beach, 1972) that show that children's reading interests vary according
to sex, age, and grade. Although researchers reported that both sexes enjoy
similar books when they are younger, they pointed out that the interests of
boys and girls begin to diverge between 10 and 13 years of age. By adolescence, most boys prefer adventure stories, and the majority of girls like

romance or modern realistic fiction (Schlager, 1974). Clearly, the children's gender and physical and emotional development, as well as the shaping forces of society, affect their reading interests. The research appeared to fit perfectly what I observed in Michael and his friends. At first I wondered why they were so interested in fantasy, then I discovered that although the stories were different from each other in a variety of ways, they were all similar in some ways to the Prydain stories.

HERO STORIES: SOME PARALLELS

In *The Book of Three* (Alexander, 1964) the first of the Prydain novels, Taran, a foundling who has become an assistant pig keeper, sets out on a series of adventures to discover his identity. The book relates his unsuccessful search for Hen Wen, a magic, oracular pig, who can give him the information he desires about his parents. In the second book of the series, *Taran Wanderer* (Alexander, 1967), the hero struggles to save Prydain from evil powers and uses magic to defeat its enemy. *The Black Cauldron* (Alexander, 1965), the third book in the series, tells how Taran finds and destroys a missing kettle in which the dread "cauldron born," mute, deathless creatures, are created from bodies found on the battlefield. When Taran loses his closest companions, he learns that to be a man among men, he must be loyal and responsible. The third book of the series, *The Castle of Llyr* (Alexander, 1966), relates his adventures on his way to the island of Mona, where Princess Eilonwy will be taught how to be a proper princess. When she is kidnapped, Taran experiences a series of breathtaking escapades and at last locates her. Finally, in *The High King* (Alexander, 1968) he again tries to find his own identity. Although he never learns who his parents were, he does discover that we must make ourselves and that greatness is a matter not of birth but of responsible choices. By undertaking noble tasks and carrying them out successfully, he has become a man of consequence.

I also observed that when viewed as separate novels, Taran's quests appear to be a series of adventures about a young man's developing maturity, but when compared with other high fantasies (see the matrix in Table 13.1), the stories suddenly take on additional meaning. It becomes clear that the Prydain novels share certain distinctive features with other high-fantasy hero stories.

Every hero in the matrix lives through experiences similar to those of Taran. With the exception of Menolly in *Dragonsong* (McCaffrey, 1976), the heroes lack important information about their births. They set out on quests to correct a wrong and to discover their own identities. Almost all of them have access to magic in the fight against evil; and once successful, all of them return home ready to help others.

Table 13.1   Hero stories in high fantasy

Story	Unknown birth	Quest	Magical powers	Good/Evil	Win
Westmark (Alexander)	X	X	X	X	X
A Wizard of Earthsea (LeGuin)	X	X	X	X	X
The Dark is Rising (Cooper)	X	X	X	X	X
Dragonsong (McCaffrey)		X	X	X	X
The Hero and the Crown (McKinley)	X	X	X	X	X

I also observed that the heroes show a strong family resemblance to protagonists from a variety of other media, for example, to movies such as *Indiana Jones and the Temple of Doom, Superman,* and *Batman,* to mention only a few; some of them, like Superman and Batman, drawn from cartoons.

Superman is an example of such a hero. Born on a planet that is far more advanced than Earth, he brings many social and technical advances with him. He divides his time between a newspaper job, where he is known as Clark Kent, and his secret Superman role. He appears to have two distinctive personalities. At the newspaper he is an ordinary young man leading an ordinary life. If anything, he is somewhat fearful of danger. But whenever society or an individual is in trouble, he changes costumes and appearance (usually in a telephone booth) and emerges into what appears to be a magical world where he can perform miraculous deeds. As Superman, he is unafraid of powerful forces of evil and frequently saves the world from near extinction after a series of seemingly miraculous deeds: he moves high-rise buildings, flies without the help of an airplane, and regularly saves people in distress. Although often near death, he always triumphs. The matrix in Table 13.2 shows that superheroes of the movies and cartoons share the same qualities as the heroes of high fantasy.

Like high-fantasy heroes, most of the movie and cartoon heroes were born under mysterious circumstances, they set out on a quest and succeed under conditions that can only be considered miraculous, and they fight evil and win (usually after an exciting chase). In short, movie and cartoon heroes resemble heroic figures from high fantasy so closely that one might be viewed as an imitation of the other.

Writers are often influenced by other literary works. High fantasy, for example, frequently appears to be influenced by Tolkien's *Lord of the Rings.*

Table 13.2 Modern hero stories found in recent, popular movies

Story	Unknown birth	Quest	Magical powers	Good/Evil	Win
Indiana Jones and the Temple of Doom		X	X	X	X
The Princess Bride	X	X	X	X	X
Superman	X	X	X	X	X
Batman	X	X	X	X	X

But the family roots of high fantasy and adventure are far older than Tolkien's stories or any other modern literature. Many modern hero stories show a marked family resemblance to the legends of King Arthur and *The Mabinogian,* ancient myths from Wales and Cornwall. Modern hero stories also resemble ancient Greek and Roman hero myths. In fact, they are remarkably like numerous other hero stories that have been told throughout human history.

Perseus, the Greek hero, is a striking example. Like his modern counterparts, Perseus grows up unsure of his identity. He is the son of Danaë, whose father, King Acrisius, imprisons her in a tower after an oracle tells him that a son born to her will kill the king. After Zeus, the king of the gods, comes to her prison tower in a shower of golden rain, Perseus is born of their union and King Acrisius throws mother and child into the sea in a wooden box. The two drift aimlessly across the water and eventually reach Seriphos, where Dictys offers them safety and adopts Perseus.

At age 15, Perseus sets out on a quest to protect his mother from the tyrant, Polydectes, king of Seriphos, who wants to marry her. When Polydectes dares Perseus to bring him the snake-covered head of the Gorgon Medusa, the boy takes on the task—even though he knows that anyone who looks directly at Medusa will immediately turn to stone.

To complete his mission, Perseus does exactly what modern superheroes do: he enters a special enchanted world when the goddess Athena gives him a magic sword that kills the monster and Hermes gives him a pair of sandals that help him to move with superhuman speed across the world. With the help of these powerful supernatural objects, Perseus kills Medusa and returns to his homeland where he kills his grandfather, King Acrisius, then becomes king and marries Andromeda. He has saved his mother and removed a tyrant from office.

Perseus resembles not only modern heroes, but also other ancient heroes of mythology, as can be seen in the matrix in Table 13.3. All of the heroes from ancient literature were born under mysterious conditions, all of them set out on quests and succeeded in completing their tasks (in part because they had magical help), all of them fought for the good, and all of

Table 13.3   Heroes in myths, legends, and the Bible

Story	Unknown birth	Quest	Magical powers	Good/Evil	Win
King Arthur	X	X	X	X	X
Jason	X	X	X	X	X
Perseus	X	X	X	X	X
Odysseus	X	X	X	X	X
Aeneas	X	X	X	X	X
Prometheus	X	X	X	X	X
Moses	X	X	X	X	X

them won. Every one of the ancient heroes, in other words, had essentially the same experiences.

Although it came as a surprise to me that all of the heroes are alike, I am in no way the only person to notice the similarities between mythological heroes. In his book, *The Hero with a Thousand Faces* (1973), Joseph Campbell describes their quests as follows:

> The hero ventures forth from the world of common day into a region of supernatural wonder: fabulous forces are there encountered and a decisive victory is won: the hero comes back from this mysterious adventure with the power to bestow boons on his fellow man. (p. 30)

Campbell also points out that the heroes and their quests are so similar that they can reasonably be called one "hero with a thousand faces." Thus, even though their stories come from a variety of cultures and times; even though some are written as novels, others as cartoons, movies, legends, or myths; and even though the stories may have different settings, characters, or details; hero tales are essentially stories about the same heroes.

A HERO WITH A THOUSAND FACES, AND THE RITES OF PASSAGE

According to Campbell, preadolescents and adolescents are fascinated by hero stories because the quests described in the stories are metaphors for rites of passage, for events that celebrate a turning point in life. Throughout history all peoples have celebrated rites of passage in their own lives and the lives of their children. An adolescent about to enter adulthood participates in the distinctive rituals of his or her culture. Long ago, Native Americans fasted and waited for a vision; many killed their first game or tried to make contact with a force not usually accessible to ordinary people. Our parents and grandparents celebrated the turning points in their lives with rituals of one kind or another, for example, confirmation in church, bar- or bat-mitzvah in synagogue, or graduation ceremonies in high school. Once young people had proven themselves, they became full members of the community. Such formal rituals symbolize an individual's transition from one stage of life to another.

Today, although we still celebrate rites of passage in our lives, we do not do so universally. Few, if any, Native Americans seek a special vision; although children celebrate graduation from high school and are frequently confirmed in church or bar or bat mitzvahed in synagogue, the ceremony does not necessarily mean that the youngster will take on the duties of adulthood. For example, although most young people attend high school graduations, the ceremony does not always mark the beginning of adulthood because many move on to university and four more years of dependency.

In the absence of universal rites of passage, young people often seek alternatives to define the roles they hope to take on as adults. For them, high-fantasy hero stories are intensely interesting because they are metaphors for experiences they would like to have, germs from which they can generate daydreams and set concrete goals. Thus high fantasies, as well as movies about superheroes, offer safe flights of fancy that become symbols or guides for readers or viewers as they carve out real-life goals. Drawn to, yet frightened by, the prospects of their own futures, young adults use high-fantasy hero stories to work through their own dreams, feelings, and goals.

HIGH FANTASY: A SECRET OPENING TO THE RING OF MYTH

High-fantasy stories mean so much to some young readers, that teachers in the fifth through ninth grades have an opportunity to harness their pupils' enthusiasm for heroes and adventures while introducing them to a variety of hero stories beyond high fantasy. The children who enjoy high fantasy and films about superheroes will enjoy ancient hero myths from Greece, Rome, Celtic England, and Scandinavia, to mention only a few. As the group reads, the teacher can point out that hero stories in myth and legend are similar to modern ones in novels and movies and that both old and new heroes embody the same experiences and symbolize the same rites of passage.

Children who compare hero stories from different eras will profit from such a program in a number of ways. First, they will be enthusiastic about their assignments, for they will be reading stories they already enjoy. Second, once they understand the relationship between ancient myths and modern stories, they are more likely to enjoy the old tales even though they have never heard them before. Third, with help from their teachers, they may come to understand the tales at many levels: as rousing adventures, as quests for improving the lot of mankind, and as metaphors of their own personal fantasies, dreams, and ambitions.

Teachers can then open another door that gives their pupils a deeper insight into literature in general. While helping their charges come to understand that hero stories are metaphors for rites of passage, teachers can also show the boys and girls that stories, which originally appeared in ancient folklore, may pop up again and again because the human condition always remains the same. Because young men frequently see themselves as heroes and life as a quest, generation after generation come to understand hero stories in one genre or another as metaphors for their own plans and dreams. In Campbell's words, the children may even learn

> that myth is the secret opening through which the inexhaustible energies of the cosmos pour into human cultural manifestations: religions, philosophies, arts, the social forms of primitive and historic man, prime discoveries in science and technology, the very dreams that blister sleep, boil up from the basic magic ring of myth. (p. 3)

I don't believe Michael, my son, ever came to see that the stories he enjoyed so much were updated versions of ancient myths, or that they were part of a grand tradition in literature. He enjoyed each story as a separate adventure unrelated to others, and then moved on to science fiction as he prepared to become a scientist. In a way his experience is typical. Although his teachers generally tried to introduce myths to his class, they did not mention that the old tales are significant parts of literary traditions.

It's a pity; he would have learned that his beloved tales had roots that went back to ancient Greece, that they have appeared and reappeared throughout history, and that modern authors merely changed the tales to suit themselves and the times in which they live. He also would have learned that the myths are about young people like himself, and that the remote heroes of mythology with strange names and stranger gods are similar to him. The high fantasies would then have become a secret opening to the ring of myth for him.

REFERENCES

Alexander, L. (1964) *The Book of Three.* New York: Holt, Rinehart and Winston.
Alexander, L. (1966) *The Castle of Llyr.* New York: Holt, Rinehart and Winston.

Alexander, L. (1967). *The Black Cauldron*. New York: Holt, Rinehart and Winston.

Alexander, L. (1968) *The High King*. New York: Holt, Rinehart and Winston.

Campbell, J. (1949/1968). *The hero with a thousand faces*. Bollingen Series XVII. Princeton, NJ: Princeton University Press.

Frye, N. (1964). *The educated imagination*. Bloomington: Indiana University Press.

Greenlaw, M. J., & Wielan, O. P. (1979). Reading interests revisited. *Language Arts, 56*, 432–434.

Huus, H. (1964). Interpreting Research in Children's Literature. In *Children, books and reading* (p. 125). Newark, DE: International Reading Association.

Purves, A., & Beach, R. (1972). *Literature and the reader: Research in response to literature*. Urbana, IL: National Council of Teachers of English.

Schlager, N. M. (1974). "Developmental Factors Influencing Children's Responses to Literature." (Doctoral dissertation, Claremont Graduate School)

BIBLIOGRAPHY

Hero Stories in the Movies

Davis, P., & Panzer, W. (Producers). (1984). *Highlander* [Film]. Los Angeles: Home Box Office/ Cannon.

Di Laurentis, D. (Producer). (1980). *Flash Gordon* [Film]. Los Angeles: Universal.

Donner, Richard. (Producer). (1978). *Superman* [Film]. Burbank, CA: Warner.Fries, C., & Goodman, D. (Producer). (1981). *Spiderman* [Film]. Prism.

Lucas, G. (Producer). (1981). *Raiders of the lost ark*. [Film]. Los Angeles: Paramount.

Lucas, G. (Producer). (1989). *Indiana Jones and the last crusade* [Film]. Los Angeles: Paramount.

Peters, J., & Guber, P. (Producers). (1989). *Batman* [Film]. Burbank, CA: Warner.

Scheineman, A. (Producer). (1987). *The princess bride* [Film]. Los Angeles: Fox.

Watts, R. (Producer). (1984). *Indiana Jones and the temple of doom* [Film]. Los Angeles: Paramount.

Hero Stories in Myths

Bryson, B. (1967). *Gilgamesh, a man's first story*. New York: Holt, Rinehart & Winston.

Carlin, E. (1960). *The song of Roland*. Illustrated by Leonard Everett Fisher. New York: Random House.

Chant, J. (1983). *The high king*. Illustrated by George Sharp. New York: Bantam.

Church, A. J. (1906/1907/1967). *The iliad and the odyssey of Homer*. Illustrated by Eugene Karlin. New York: Macmillan.

Colum, P. (1984). *The children's Homer: the adventures of Odysseus and the tale of Troy*. Illustrated by N. C. Wyeth. New York: Scribner's.

Evslin, B. (1984). *Hercules*. Illustrated by Joseph A. Smith. New York: Morrow.

Evslin, B. (1985). *The adventures of Ulysses.* New York: Scholastic.

Evslin, B. (1988). *The Trojan War.* New York: Scholastic.

Evslin, B., Evslin, D., & Hoopes, N. (1970/1988). *Heroes and monsters of Greek myths.* Illustrated by William Hunter. New York: Scholastic.

Evslin, B., Evslin, D., & Hoopes, N. (1988). *The Greek gods.* New York: Scholastic.

Green, R. L. (1958). *Tales of the Greek heroes.* London: Penguin.

Green, R. L. (1960). *Heroes of Greece and Troy.* London: The Bodley Head.

Green, R. L. (1965). *A book of myths.* Illustrated by Joan Kiddell-Monroe. New York: Dutton.

Hodges, M. (1972). *The gorgan's head.* Illustrated by Charles Mikolaycak. Boston: Little, Brown.

Hodges, M. (1973). *The other world: myths of the Celts.* Illustrated by Eros Kieth. New York: Farrar, Straus & Giroux.

Hodges, M. (1984). *St George and the dragon.* Illustrated by Trina Schart Hyman. Boston: Little, Brown.

Holland, K. C. (1965). *Havelock the Dane.* Illustrated by Brian Wildsmith. New York: Dutton.

Jones, T. (1983). *The sage of Erik the Viking.* London: Viking Penguin.

Lanier, S. (1880). *The boy's King Arthur.* Illustrated by N. C. Wyeth. New York: Scribner's.

Lister, R. (1988a). *The legend of King Arthur.* New York: Doubleday.

Lister, R. (1988b). *The odyssey.* New York: Doubleday.

Low, A. (1985). *The Macmillan book of Greek gods and heroes.* Illustrated by Arvis Stewart. New York: Macmillan.

McGovern, A. (1970). *Robin Hood of Sherwood Forest.* Illustrated by Tracy Sugarman. New York: Scholastic.

Malcolmson, A. (1947). *The song of Robin Hood.* Music arranged by Grace Castagnetta. Illustrated by Virginia Lee Burton. New York: Houghton Mifflin.

Murkerji, D. G. (1930). *Rama, the hero of India.* Illustrated by Edgar Parin d'Aulaire. New York: Dutton.

Naden, C. J. (1981). *Theseus and the minotaur.* New York: Troll.

Picard, B. L. (1955). *Stories of King Arthur and his knights.* Illustrated by Roy Morgan. New York: Walck.

Picard, B. L. (1960). *The iliad of Homer.* Illustrated by Joan Kiddell-Monroe. New York: Walck.

Picard, B. L. (1962). *The odyssey of Homer retold.* New York: Walck.

Picard, B. L. (1969). *Hero tales from the minotaur.* Illustrated by Gay Galsworthy. London: Penguin.

Pyle, H. (1946). *The merry adventures of Robin Hood.* New York: Scribner's.

Richardson, I. M. (1984). *Odysseus and the cyclops.* New York: Troll.

Serraillier, I. (1963). *The way of danger: The story of Theseus.* Illustrated by William Stobbs. New York: Walck.

Serraillier, I. (1964). *The clashing rocks: The story of Jason.* Illustrated by William Stubbs. New York: Walck.

Serraillier, I. (1970). *The gorgon's head: The story of Perseus.* Illustrated by Rocco Negri. New York: Walck.

Sutcliffe, R. (1980). *The light behind the forest: The quest for the Holy Grail*. New York: Dutton.
White, T. H. (1939). *The sword in the stone*. New York: Putnam.
Williams, J. (1968). *Sword of King Arthur*. Illustrated by Louis Glanzman. New York: Crowell.

Hero Stories in High Fantasy

Alexander, L. (1964). *The book of three*. New York: Holt, Rinehart, & Winston.
Alexander, L. (1965). *The black cauldron*. New York: Holt, Rinehart, & Winston.
Alexander L. (1966). *The castle of Llyr*. New York: Holt, Rinehart, & Winston.
Alexander, L. (1967). *Taran wanderer*. New York: Holt, Rinehart, & Winston.
Alexander, L. (1968). *The high king*. New York: Holt, Rinehart, & Winston.
Alexander, L. (1982a). *The foundling and other tales of Prydain*. New York: Dell.
Alexander, L. (1982b). *The kestrel*. New York: Dutton.
Alexander, L. (1984). *The beggar queen*. New York: Dutton.
Alexander, L. (1981). *Westmark*. New York: Dutton.
Cooper, S. (1966). *Over sea, under stone*. Illustrated by Marjorie Gill. New York: Harcourt Brace Jovanovich.
Cooper, S. (1973). *The dark is rising*. Illustrated by Alan E. Cober. New York: Atheneum.
Cooper, S. (1974a). *Greenwitch*. New York: Atheneum.
Cooper, S. (1974b). *The grey king*. New York: Atheneum.
Cooper, S. (1977). *Silver on the tree*. New York: Atheneum.
Garner, A. (1967). *Elidor*. New York: Walck.
LeGuin, U. (1968). *A wizard of earthsea*. Illustrated by Ruth Robbins. Boston: Parnassus.
LeGuin, U. (1971). *The tombs of Atuan*. Illustrated by Gail Garraty. New York: Atheneum.
LeGuin, U. (1972). *The farthest shore*. Illustrated by Gail Garraty. New York: Atheneum.
McCaffrey, A. (1976). *Dragonsong*. Illustrated by Laura Lydecker. New York: Atheneum.
McCaffrey, A. (1977). *Dragonsinger*. New York: Atheneum.
McCaffrey, A. (1979). *Dragondrums*. Illustrated by Fred Marcelino. New York: Atheneum.
McKillop, P. A. (1976). *The riddle master of Hed*. New York: Atheneum.
McKillop, P. A. (1977). *The heir of sea and fire*. New York: Atheneum.
McKillop, P. A. (1979). *The harpist in the wind*. New York: Atheneum.
McKinley, R. (1982). *The blue sword*. New York: Greenwillow.
McKinley, R. (1985). *The hero and the crown*. New York: Greenwillow.

TRY THIS

If you are working with younger children:

Read your class an adventure story like M. Hodges' *Saint George and the dragon* (illustrated by Trina Schart Hyman; Boston: Little, Brown, 1984), and show them a movie or cartoon like *Batman* or *Superman*. After they are acquainted with a number of stories, ask the boys and girls to draw a map with pictures of the places where their heroes went. They should also show what the heroes brought back and how they improved the world.

If you are working with older children:

1. Show the class one of the movies on videotape like those listed in the preceding Bibliography under "Hero Stories in the Movies." Ask the following questions to help children understand repeated features in the hero stories:

   - Who are the hero's parents?
   - What tasks does the hero undertake?
   - Why does he or she do so?
   - Describe the hero's adventures?
   - Does the hero appear to be in a magical world? Why? How did the hero achieve his or her goal? Did the hero have the help of magical forces?
   - What gift or boon did the hero bring back?

2. Read a high-fantasy hero story. Ask the same questions as those listed above. Fill out a matrix like the one listed below. Ask what the stories have in common.

Hero/myth matrix

Story	Unknown birth	Quest	Magical powers	Good/Evil	Win

3. Compare hero fantasies and myths with hero cartoons, if available. Compare the heroes and the stories. Are they alike or different from each other? Continue to fill out the matrix.
4. Ask the children to read a high-fantasy book and then a number of hero myths. Continue to fill out the matrix, which remains on display.
5. Ask the class why they think that the heroes have so many similar experiences. Encourage the children to guess.
6. Explain that the mission itself is a metaphor for the experiences all young people have as they become adults. Ask what the class thinks the stories may mean about becoming an adult. Ask what the pupils in the class think they share with the heroes in the myths and high fantasies. Do any of the children in the class think that they are like the heroes and heroines? (Accept any answer. Help the class understand that the stories are metaphors or symbols for rites of passage.)
7. Ask the students to write a hero story:

   • Ask everyone in the class to introduce themselves to someone else. They should tell the other person something important about themselves: who their parents are, where they are from, what they like to do, what they want to do after they finish school.
   • Ask everyone to write a story in any form they like—a cartoon, a play, a short story, a myth—about their own personal quests. They should tell what they will do to make the world a better place.
   • Ask the students to write a first draft, then revise and edit their compositions.

Finally, place the stories in a "class book."

—G.B.

ABOUT THE CONTRIBUTORS

Naomi Barnett is the author of numerous teaching materials and of 18 children's books, including several in the *Let's Go* series, which she edited for Putnam. She has worked as an elementary school teacher and for a variety of publishers as an editor. Some of her most outstanding articles include "Magical Caddy" in *Elementary English* and "Equality through Integration" (Anti-Defamation League). In recent years she has taught both reading and writing in several colleges. She received her Ed.D. from St. John's University in New York City.

Gloria T. Blatt, associate professor of children's literature and language arts at Oakland University, teaches courses in children's literature and language arts. The author of many articles on children's literature, oral language development, expressive movement, and creative writing, she also wrote *It's Your Move* (Teachers College Press) with Jean Cunningham. She has taught both elementary and secondary school and also works as a consultant in children's literature and language arts. She received her Ph.D. in children's literature at Michigan State University.

Bette Bosma, professor of children's literature at Calvin College, is the author of *Fairy Tales, Fables, Legends and Myths: Using Folk Literature in your Classroom* (Teachers College Press), at present in its second edition. Before joining the faculty at Calvin College, she was a middle school reading consultant and taught at every grade from kindergarten to ninth grade. She conducts numerous workshops throughout the country on getting children and books together. She earned her Ph.D. at Michigan State University in children's literature, reading, and language arts.

Patricia J. Cianciolo, a nationally known authority on children's literature and reading, is the author of numerous articles on children's and adolescent literature that have appeared in national journals like *Language Arts* and *English Journal,* as well as *Top of the News* and the *Journal of Personnel and Guidance.* She is also the author of *Picture Books for Children* (American Library Association) and *Illustrations of Children's Books* (W. C.

Brown), both widely used texts on picture books. She has done research on children's responses to literature and has been the Chair of the Newbery and Caldecott Award Committees. She was a team leader for the children's choices project sponsored by the International Reading Association and Children's Book Council and has also chaired the Batchelder Award for Literature in Translation. She received her Ph.D. from Ohio State University.

Sheila Fitzgerald, professor of education at Michigan State University, is a specialist in language arts. A popular speaker, she often gives professional talks on language arts instruction and political issues associated with quality education. She has written many articles on teaching creative writing and is the author of the chapter on teacher evaluation in the *Handbook of Research on Teaching the English Language Arts* (IRA and NCTE) and the forthcoming chapter "Language Domain" in A *Practical Guide for Creating Developmentally Appropriate Programs in Early Childhood Education* (Merrill/Macmillan). She has been the president of the National Council of Teachers of English and the Michigan Council of Teachers of English. She received her Ph.D. from the University of Minnesota.

Don Haase is an associate professor of German and the Chair of the Department of German and Slavic Languages and Literature at Wayne State University. His work includes publications on the theory of the fantastic, fairy-tale films, the fairy tales of German exile writers and the works of Michael Ende, a German author of children's books. He has directed NEH Summer Seminars for schoolteachers on the Brothers Grimm and is the editor of the forthcoming volume on the reception of Grimm's tales (Wayne State University Press). His annotated bibliography of scholarship on Grimms' fairy tales is in progress for Garland Publications. His work has been supported by grants from Wayne State University, the National Endowment for the Humanities, and the German Academic Exchange Service.

Alethea K. Helbig, professor of English language and literature at Eastern Michigan University, teaches courses in Native American literature, mythology, folklore, the Bible as literature, and children's literature. She has written numerous articles and a number of standard texts on folklore and children's literature. Most recently, she completed *Nanabozhoo, Giver of Life* (Green Oak Press), co-edited two collections of poetry: *Straight on Till Morning* (Crowell) and *Dusk to Dawn* (Crowell) and coauthored (with Agnes Perkins) a series of critical references on award-winning fiction for children and young people including the *Dictionary of American Children's*

Fiction, 1859–1959 and the *Dictionary of American Children's Fiction, 1960–1984* (Greenwood Press). She has been named Distinguished Professor for Research and Publication at Eastern Michigan University and was the recipient of the Michigan Association of Governing Boards Award for Outstanding Faculty. She holds degrees from the University of Michigan.

Eric A. Kimmel is a professor of children's literature at Portland State University in Portland, Oregon. A popular storyteller known throughout the Great Northwest, Dr. Kimmel is also well known as a writer of children's books and of professional articles on children's literature. Some of his more recent children's books include *Anansi and the Moss-Covered Rock* (Holiday House); *The Chanukkah Guest* (Holiday House) and *Hershel and the Hanukkah Goblins* (Holiday House). His professional writing has appeared in many periodicals including *The Horn Book* and *Language Arts,* among others. He received his Ph.D. from the University of Illinois.

Margaret Read MacDonald, a storyteller, folklorist, and librarian, is the author of many standard texts on folklore and librarianship, including *One Hundred and One Skits for Children* (Shoestring Press); *The Storyteller's Source Book: A Subject, Title, and Motif Index to Folklore Collections for Children* (Neal-Schuman/Gale), for which she received an award from the American Library Association. She has worked as a children's librarian in many libraries, including ones in King County, Washington; and San Francisco. Dr. MacDonald earned a Ph.D. in folklore from the University of Indiana.

R. Craig Roney is an associate professor in elementary education at Wayne State University, where he teaches courses in children's literature, storytelling, and language arts. He has served as Chair of the Storyteller's Special Interest Group of the International Reading Association (1980–1982), Chair of the Advisory Council of the National Association for the Preservation and Perpetuation of Storytelling (1980–1982), and Chair of the Advisory Council of the National Association for the Preservation of Storytelling (1988–1989). He is currently Chair of the Committee on Storytelling of the National Council of the Teachers of English. Craig frequently conducts storytelling demonstrations and workshops in school and at regional and national conventions for various educational organizations.

Mark Workman, a Ph.D. graduate of the University of Pennsylvania in folklore, is at present an associate professor of English and Chair of the English Department at Oakland University. A very popular lecturer and a frequent speaker at conferences, he is also the author of numerous articles, including "Proverbs for the Pious and the Paranoid: The Social Use of Metaphor," "Tropes, Hopes and Dopes," in *The Journal of American Folklore* and "Narratable and Unnarratable Lives" in *Western Folklore*. He recently read a paper at the American Folklore Society: "Paradigms of Interdeterminacy."

Index